Wounded Wounders

◆

Books by A. Companion

Wounded Wounders—Stories of Men in Prison

Poignant, powerful stories of men in prison told in their own words. These are stories of wounders—themselves wounded—stories of sin, hopelessness, grace and redemption. ISBN: 0-595-17674-7

Peace and Justice Shall Embrace—Toward Restorative Justice

Unparalleled practical, biblical and human critique of the U.S. criminal justice systems, with cogent proposals and models for restorative justice reforms. A cross-reference is provided to the U.S. Catholic bishops' statement on criminal justice: *Responsibility, Rehabilitation and Restoration.* ISBN: 0-595-17654-2

These books may be ordered from iUniverse.com, Amazon.com, BN.com or your favorite bookstore.

Proceeds from the sale of these books go to Restoration House (a charitable non-profit corporation) to be established in Sacramento.

Restoration House Mission Statement

Restoration House is a faith-based ministry of Christian compassion, love and healing. We provide a transitional community for men paroled from prison.

We are committed:

- to the restorative processes of reclaiming personal dignity;
- to facing and dealing with addictive and self-destructive patterns;
- to learning practical and social living skills;
- to the transition to employment and self sufficiency as fully integrated, contributing members of society.

Wounded Wounders

Stories of Men in Prison

◆

A. Companion

Writers Club Press
San Jose New York Lincoln Shanghai

Wounded Wounders
Stories of Men in Prison

Writers Club Press
an imprint of iUniverse.com, Inc.

For information address:
iUniverse.com, Inc.
5220 S 16th, Ste. 200
Lincoln, NE 68512
www.iuniverse.com

ISBN: 0-595-17674-7

Printed in the United States of America

The Stories

Preface—The Author

I am a former Roman Catholic priest, and I am writing from prison—not as a chaplain, but as a prisoner. Unlike most of my companions here who grew up in the penal system, I entered the world of the criminal justice system at age 56, out of a professional background with all of the social and economic benefits which come with education, status in the community, and the security of a stable family.

Only now, in this context, in which my prior status and social advantages no longer open doors or guarantee privileges, and no longer protect me from the dehumanizing, cramped, cruel and crude everyday environment which prison is, have I come to understand experientially the humbling truth of "Unless you've walked in my shoes…"

Entering prison was, for me, like entering a foreign country with its own language, culture, laws, and political and economic infrastructures. I had been warned ahead of time: "keep a low profile, mind your own business, trust no one, don't disturb the racial 'ecology,' keep your back to the wall."

Still, the habits of a lifetime of ministering, as well as my naivete, kept breaking through spontaneously, as I responded to simple needs of my neighbors. I mistook smiles as friendliness, and misunderstood "friendly" conversation to be "welcome wagon" activity, rather than the sizing-up of potential prey. Slowly, the consistency of my patterns, and, I'm sure, my grandfatherly gray hair and obvious ignorance of prison ways, allowed a few to lower their defenses enough to entrust me with some of their needs.

The first level of trust was asking for material things—the loan of a soup or a dollar until canteen. Then it was requests for help reading or completing legal papers, letters to or from loved ones, or assistance with schoolwork. Bit by bit, I became aware, at least superficially, of their hurts, hopes, fears and fantasies.

Among my tattooed brothers—serving as unwitting tutors to me—I have come to experience in powerful ways that we are *all* made of the same "stuff," that we share a common flawed humanity, that we hurt and hope and fear and heal out of the same deep human needs.

The process that led to this book began out of the same unconscious condescension with which I have always reached out to "care for the less fortunate." My compassion was genuine, and my motives seemed noble—*I* have seen and felt their pain. *I* will tell the stories of my uneducated and uncultured brothers *for* them.

Even though I was now one of "them" and shared the opprobrium of "criminal," I still saw myself as different from and set apart—*they* were criminals, I was not. I was not cut from the same cloth, even if I wore the same uniform. "They" were "different from" me, and that difference left me smugly feeling "better than."

Unexpectedly, as I listened to their stories, and was entrusted with their woundedness, I found myself being drawn not only into their worlds, but also more deeply into mine.

I discovered myself hurting not only for the hurts they had borne, or those they had inflicted upon others, but for my own, as well. Through their simple, honest, uncomplicated sharing of their stories, I began to see the obfuscation, rationalization and denial in facing my own. These men not only allowed me to see the secrets of their hearts and histories, but also opened a window for me into myself. As I sought to minister to them, they unintentionally ministered to me.

While the worlds in which they grew up and lived were very different from mine, and the externals of their life experiences very foreign, as I listened to their hurts and hopes, their bungled attempts to love and find love, their fears and defenses against feeling pain, it soon became evident that we shared a common humanity, made all the more fraternal by our common brokenness.

There is much that is ugly and shameful in our worlds—both the one I left and the one in which I now live—yet, I have found much to respect and love here, where I never would have expected it. I have a new awareness of being privileged, a term I now define by the pride I feel at being called "friend" by these men with whom I share a wonderful mutuality of companionship.

Frequently, friends have sought to encourage me with "*God has put you there for a purpose.*" My response is, "*No, I put me here, but God is definitely using my presence for his purposes.*" This reality has given me meaning for being here. While in no way denying or belittling the humiliation, losses and pain—either that I've caused others, or experienced myself—this has been a time of amazing grace, and a redemptive process for me. But this is not my story. I will tell my own story at another time.

None of our stories are over yet—theirs, mine, yours. None of us know for sure what those chapters yet to be written contain. The simple hope and goal I have in offering this book is that by listening to, and walking among us wounded wounders, you might recognize enough of yourself to be able to see "brother" in the rest of us.

I am my brothers' brother, as well as a companion.

I Am Indebted to my sister, Joanne, for patiently deciphering my notes, serving as editor, and doing the computer work. I am also grateful to the friends who encouraged me in this project by their enthusiastic interest.

"Unless You've Walked in My Shoes..."

Most citizens probably presume, as I did, that an effort is made to rehabilitate prisoners, with the hope they will one day return to society as productive citizens. The truth is that the designation "Department of *Corrections*" is an Orwellian parody in itself. Prison neither "corrects" nor rehabilitates, nor does it make any serious effort to do so. By political mandate, California prisons are simply warehouses of human potential, graveyards of the human spirit. In the manner of the great black holes of outer space, prison—by its very nature and design—sucks out all that is good, hopeful and humane of the inner space of those committed to its custody.

A large majority of inmates are illiterate, or able to read and write at only a basic level. Only a small percent have salary-potential skills[1]. Most grew up on the streets, even if not gang affiliated. Eighty percent of their crimes are drug related in some way.[2]

Most inmates enter the system at an early age; many begin in junior high. They grow up physically while incarcerated, but their social and psychological development fixate at a primitive level. Prison life becomes normative. Prison values and mores become theirs. The "homies" become family.

---

1. A 1996 prison study by Educational Testing Service reported "two-thirds" of inmates lack even the most basic math and communication skills." Steven T. Jones, *New Times* (San Luis Obispo), 26 Apr. 1998:10.
2. "Illegal drugs and alcohol helped lead to the imprisonment of four out of five inmates in the nation's prisons and jails...," from a Jan. 8, 1998 report, National Center on Addiction and Substance Abuse (Columbia Univ.), The Sacramento Bee, 9 Jan.1998.

While the physical facilities of each prison are different, the basic environment and lifestyle are similar. Not much distinguishes one day from another: the schedule is the same, the menus predictable, the scenery never changes. The routine creates a rhythm of order, as well as monotony. Over a period of time, the routine and rhythms become "normal"—that is the process of institutionalization.

Many inmates become so institutionalized they become incapable of functioning anywhere else. This is a blessing for those who will spend most or all of their lives here, but one more handicap for those who eventually leave.

*   *   *   *   *

"Doing time" is the ultimate reality and challenge for every prisoner. One's sense of time changes here. There are no weekends at grandma's, no going out for beer and pizza, no summer vacations, the routine is fixed, the scenery never changes. Those with determinate sentences are able to count the days, months and years left to serve. They are able to dream, plan and work toward other possibilities. "Lifers,"[3] however, have to find some kind of meaning and purpose within the limitations of these walls, and the endless repetition of sameness.

Privacy doesn't exist. An inmate is always present, always under observation, always surrounded by others. Except in rare circumstances, each man shares a small living space with at least one other. Most double cells were built for one person. The stainless steel combination sink-

---

3. "Lifer" refers to inmates serving indeterminate sentences, such as 7-to-life or 25-to-life. They become *eligible for consideration* for parole after most of the minimum number of years have been served. For political reasons, in practice, many inmates serve life terms regardless of merit or rehabilitation.

toilet takes up part of the little movement space, which is often as little as 4' x 10'. There is usually a small desk and one chair. Personal TVs and radios are usually allowed. Other living units are dorms in which up to a hundred men (or more) are crammed together in rows of bunk beds, each man having a small locked storage space for personal belongings. Nothing can be left out—there is no "honor among thieves." Turning off the light, listening to the radio, using the toilet, smoking, and other mundane aspects of life, become communal issues to be negotiated and shared, as well as sources of argument and tension. In many prisons, it is not uncommon to be on lockdown for weeks at a time, confined to the cells with an hour (or no time) for exercise, a shower 2-3 times a week.

Theoretically, smoking is forbidden in the cells, but, for the most part, the ban is ignored by both inmates and staff. Since 90% of inmates smoke, it is almost impossible for non-smokers to avoid secondhand smoke, even outside.

Men from different racial groups are not usually assigned together in double cells, except by mutual agreement, while dorms are mixed racially. The person with whom you spend most of the day only inches apart can be thirty years older or younger, have AIDS or hepatitis-C, be crazy or threatening, thoughtful or thoughtless, clean or a slob. A compatible cellie makes life bearable, and sometimes provides friendship. A bad cellie is excruciating, and exacerbates all the other pressures of prison life.

* * * * *

Everything about prison is a hassle. Every day is punctuated by standing in line for one thing or another, showing IDs, getting permissions, responding to loudspeaker announcements, rushing through meals before the allotted time runs out. Mail is censored both coming in and going out. The availability of telephone calls is sporadic. Calls are monitored, and conversations are interrupted by recorded warnings: "This call originates from a California correctional institution." All calls are collect. If no one answers, there is no way to leave a message.

Library and chapel access is limited, but usually available. Sick call, however, can mean sitting on a bench for several hours waiting to be seen by a doctor or nurse.

In most cases, visiting is done in crowded visiting areas. Except for a greeting and goodbye kiss and hug, holding hands is the only sharing of affection allowed. Personal matters needing to be aired, tears, shared prayer, arguments are all on public display. Since most prisons are in remote rural areas, and prisoners are frequently moved from one prison to another, loved ones are often too far away to visit. Inmates with spouses and children have little meaningful part in their family's life and the separation often leads to estrangement or dissolution.

*　*　*　*　*

By law, all inmates who are physically and psychologically capable, are required to work at least a 35 hour week, or to be in school or vocational training programs. Men who test below seventh grade level academically are required to go to school at least until they reach that level of competency. In reality, because of overcrowding, there are at least a third again more inmates than jobs, and educational and vocational programs continue to dwindle, as funding is switched to custody needs.

Men often wait up to eight months before being assigned to work or school. Prison jobs pay from nothing to $52.00 a month; those working in industries can earn over a $100.00 a month. For many, prison work is their only source of income for canteen use. Otherwise, the state provides only a weekly razor, bar of soap and roll of toilet paper.

* * * * *

Violence among inmates is usually sparked by unpaid drug deals (drugs, brought in by staff or visitors, are readily available in prison) or gambling debts, or connected to gang or racial conflicts. For the most part, men associate primarily with those in their own racial groups. In most prisons, to do otherwise is to set up one's self for harassment or sticking (knifing). Even members of different gangs within the same racial group don't socialize for the same reason. Often areas of the yard "belong" to particular groups in ways similar to the neighborhood turf on the streets. It is painfully (often literally) difficult for a man to break away from his gang affiliation to pursue a different way of life. There are gang connections in every prison, as well as back home. The group demands loyalty, being isolated is vulnerability. Those who manage to break away, usually have to fight their way out.

* * * * *

"Respect" is the underlying code of prison life, as well as the keeper of its peace. As lived and practiced, it is actually a form of ritualized fear. "Respect" covers everything from what is said and done deliberately, as well as how one responds to accidentally bumping into someone in the corridor, or how one man looks at another in the yard.

The always-simmering hostility between rival gangs or racial groups is kept from boiling over by an exaggerated "politeness," references to enemies as "gentlemen," and a form of diplomatic negotiations.

"Respect" is the delicate line that allows the correctional officers to maintain order. The successful guards are those who accomplish the delicate balance between being "in charge" and being "decent." Inmates categorize guards into three groups: decents, jerks, haters. For the most part, the officers are under-trained and under-educated, and those who mingle among the inmates are unarmed. They are always aware that they "disrespect" an inmate to their own risk.

"Respect" does not extend to child molesters or "rats" ("squealers," "snitches"—those who report to the authorities any personal harm done to themselves, or contraband or other violations by their fellow inmates). It is always open season on them.

* * * * *

The sexual dimension of prison life is not easily explained to out-siders. Heterosexual men confined for years in a crowded, all male, macho world either adapt to a celibate lifestyle, a fantasy life of self-gratification, or a pretend "marriage" or "girlfriend" from among the homosexual or transgender inmates. Active homosexuals pair or group up, or allow themselves to be "kept" (financially supported for sexual favors) as the lover ("punk," "queer") of someone else. The term "gay" is not in prison vocabulary, and few are offended at being called homosexuals or homos. Publicly holding hands, caressing and sharing other forms of courtship are done without harassment. What might be thought to be "respect" or "tolerance" is more accurately a laissez-faire atmosphere of "If you pretend it's real and okay for me, I'll do the same for you."

* * * * *

Intimacy—understood as a mutual experience of deep self-revelation between two persons—is not easily found anywhere. Many individuals, marriages and friendships flounder along for years seeking it, missing the mark, and settling for "Brand X" substitutes, which do not quench this innate human need, but, instead, only intensify the hunger.

Most men in prison have never known intimacy in the meaning given above. Most aren't even consciously aware that it is possible between two persons. Nonetheless, many are here for having sought it in the most dysfunctional ways, or for having acted out in some angry and destructive way for lack of it.

There is little in prison to foster intimacy—there was little in the families in which many inmates grew up, or the relationships with their "old ladies" or "bitches"—but much here to exacerbate the negative consequences of its deprivation.

＊ ＊ ＊ ＊ ＊

Here, physical survival is the basic priority of every day. It requires constant vigilance, the projection of toughness, and suspicion of the intentions, motives and movements of "the others." Any sign of weakness or vulnerability is an invitation to exploitation. Even the simplest acts of kindness or generosity are presumed to contain some kind of "you owe me" hook.

In relation to each other, prisoners learn to survive by conning, subterfuge, barter or battery. Most inmates fear most other inmates. To protect oneself physically—especially if young, weak or a "pretty boy"—it is often necessary to develop a muscular physique, or to be part of a group or gang. The most vulnerable—young, weak, alone—sometimes buy protection with money, goods or sexual favors.

In relation to the system, inmates are reinforced in their self-images as losers, and less-than-humans. They are not allowed to make adult choices or decisions, to be right, to speak up in their own defense, even in the face of the most egregious injustices or absurdities. They are yelled at for all kinds of reasons—as well as no reason at all—given arbitrary and disproportionate punishments for insignificant infractions, and constantly subject to humiliation and search. Here in "law and order" land, rules are enforced at the whim of each officer, and often are applied differently to different inmates. While there are procedures for filing complaints, inmates are aware that challenging one officer is attacking them all.

To protect one's self psychologically from the degradation, dehumanization, fear and loneliness, which pervade and define prison existence, most inmates build high and thick walls against feelings, and project tough, "don't mess with me" exteriors. For those who lived on the streets early in life, these processes are already well developed before prison. Here, though, whatever youthful innocence or ignorance left is quickly expunged. Here, every man is an island adrift in an amoral subculture, in which having a conscience is perceived as weakness, and showing compassion leaves one vulnerable. Over time, this hardened, defensive, fearful posture leads to personal disintegration.

* * * * *

In August 1999, there were 162,000 prisoners incarcerated in California's thirty-three prisons (an increase of 2,420 over one year), 45,726 employees of the Department of Corrections, and a 1999-2000 budget of $4,609,000,000. The inmate population was 93% male, 34% Hispanic, 31% black, 30% white, 5% other. Their average age, 34.[4]

There are four security levels into which prisons and inmates are classified, with Level I being the lowest. Each living area within a prison is controlled at one of these levels, although individuals assigned there may be classified at a different level for administrative reasons.

Wounded Wounders was written in 1997 and 1998 (and updated in 2000) at a Level III prison. Represented within its population is every crime for which people are imprisoned, from parole violation to murder. There is no such person as a "typical criminal."

Lacking use of a tape recorder, I took notes at a series of at least six sessions with each man, as we sat in the yard, as the activities and noises of prison life went on around us. Universally, after a hesitating start, the experience was cathartic. Two men told me they had never opened up to anyone before, and how healing it was to have someone just listen to them without judging them. Twice sessions ended when it became emotionally too difficult for them to continue.

At the end of our last session, Armando articulated what all the others also expressed to me in some way:

> *"Don't quit what you are doing. There are too many people who need someone to talk to, and to let out all their angers and fears, and there isn't anyone.*

---

4. Institution and Parole Population and Movements Summary, California Dept of Corrections, August 1999.

"One of the important things about doing this was that it allowed me to release a lot of painful feelings and things I needed to let out. I don't care if it is ever part of a book. I see you as a friend who was willing to listen. I feel like a big load has been taken away. That you were willing to sit and listen, no matter what, means a lot—it means a lot just to have someone to listen, being able to trust someone with things so personal."

In every case, when the first drafts were returned for review and correction, the response was tears. Each man was given a copy of his story, and each was eager to share it with someone. Having had someone give value to their histories, and being able to possess them on paper, gave a sense of meaning and value to their lives.

A sincere effort was made to capture the words of the storytellers, and to tell each story as it was shared. They, therefore, read somewhat like diary entries—choppy, not always flowing from thought to thought, not fully developed. Prison and street "lingo," and the grammar and speech patterns common to certain ethnic groups have been modified, while trying to keep the unique personality of each storyteller. By their choice, the names of the storytellers are real. All other persons mentioned are real, but their names are fictitious.

Each of the stories raises corollary issues related to the justice and corrections systems, and touch upon public policy. As epilogues, I have added my personal observations and critiques of "the system," which is, more often than not, part of the problems rather than the solutions. I treat "the system" in depth in my second prison book: *Peace and Justice Shall Embrace.*

* * * * *

It is out of this milieu that these stories come. These are stories of wounders, themselves wounded. There is more to each of our stories, though, than our covers.

Lewis—"It Was Sex, Drugs and Rock'n Roll"

I was afraid of Lewis at first. I was new to prison and the tier, and he fit my stereotype of "criminal": black, muscular, scarred, cocky walk, and a "Big Bad Wolf" smile, made all the more sinister by a gold tooth. Even now, it is that smile—like that of the Cheshire Cat's—which hangs disembodied in my memories of Lewis.

I don't remember how we actually met, or what led to any exchange of conversation. I suspect he was prowling the tier looking for a loan of coffee or tobacco—neither of which I use or had. That's how I met a lot of men on the tier. In any case, the relationship initially developed around his borrowing soups or canteen scrip.[5] He was always smiling whenever we made contact, and he was pleasant, but also on guard. He would never come right out and ask for whatever it was he needed, but would ask in a casual, conspiratorial way, *"Can you help a man in need"* or *"What are the chances a man could get a soup?"*

It wasn't easy to really converse with Lewis. Everything was kept light, friendly and superficial. He approached out of practical need, not for companionship. Except for his daily hour of working out on the weights, he was rarely in the yard. Most of his time was spent in his cell watching TV or reading. His workout partner was the only person with whom he seemed close, and their time together was primarily while working out. He kept his distance, and kept everyone at a distance.

---

5. Prison "funny money" used to buy sodas, candy and other canteen items.

Behind the smile and wary nature, I began to sense a melancholy void. As I became more comfortable with him, and his trust in me grew, I spent short periods talking with him about his life and situation. Bits and pieces came out—nothing profound, nothing emotive, nothing more than was required.

For some time, I had been toying with writing a book in which I'd try to capture the humanity of my companions—that which I was encountering myself, as my stereotypes and neat "categories" were confronted with more than my eyes perceived. I thought to myself, *"Maybe this is where I start?"* I asked Lewis if we could talk. He was hesitantly agreeable. I could see and feel his "caution lights" flashing. We went to the yard and sat in the bleachers. I shared my idea for *Wounded Wounders*, showed him an outline of what I had in mind, and asked if he would be willing to be my first subject. His reaction was, *"Why me?"* I told him what I had come to sense was in him—behind the smile—and that I felt he had a lot to share. He wasn't so sure his story would be of interest to anyone, but he was willing to do it, as a favor to me.

At our first session—again in the yard bleachers—I sat with my note pad and invited him to tell me about his experiences of growing up. It was a warm day with blue skies, the sounds of the yard provided the background: talking, laughing, rap and Spanish music blaring out of multiple sound boxes. He began to talk. I listened and took notes.

* * * * *

Lewis is 36. Until he joined the Navy after high school, his world was the streets of the black ghettos of St. Louis, Missouri. He is a slim, athletic 5' ll", and scarred from his life on the streets. His hair is styled in an erratic blend of dreadlocks and cornrow braids. As I've said, his smile is big, but wary.

Lewis was intense as he began to tell his story. His initial hesitancy quickly gave way to rapid-fire vignettes. I had difficulty understanding much of what he was saying, because of the black cadence and unfamiliar speech patterns. I tried not to interrupt, and waited for breaks, or shifts in the story, before going back to fill in the blanks. Doing so served as an entree to hear the story again with new perspectives and additional information. Lewis shared his memories with more rationality than emotion. His speech was strung together with *"You know what I mean?"* and *"Man."*

Unlike Lewis' initial hesitancy at the first listening session, he was eager for the next ones, even to the point of asking me when we were going to meet next. While he still told his story more with the distanced objectivity of an observer, rather than the emotive subject, it was obvious he was telling *his* story, and, doing so was having a cathartic effect on him. As he spoke about his mother, being a father, and the betrayal of a friend, the first signs of real pain began to show. His voice softened and slowed, he looked at me to see if I was able to understand, if it was okay and safe to be weak.

I don't know that it was "understanding" that was taking place within me, but I knew something was changing inside. Lewis had been introducing me to experiences and a way of life totally foreign to my own. Yet, it was on another, more profound level, that I was responding to him. I was beginning to know him in a heartfelt way, as a man, as a person who no longer seemed so unlike me. The details of our life-stories are as different as our physical characteristics and personalities, but he was reaching me in our common humanity, our common woundedness, and I was hurting for him and with him.

The physical characteristics and mannerisms that first evoked fear touching—as they did my stereotypic prejudices—no longer seemed to matter. As with clothes outgrown, they no longer seemed to fit. I was coming to know Lewis *as* Lewis. Now, the characteristics with which I identified him, and with him, were those of the heart and spirit. No longer was his story the story of a "criminal," it had become the story of someone with whom I identified, and about whom I cared.

Over the six weeks or so that our listening sessions took place, a friendship began to take root and grow. A mutual affection showed itself in an arm around the shoulders, joking back and forth, going to meals together. For the most part, though, Lewis maintained the same patterns of staying to himself, working out on the weights, watching football on TV, reading.

I discovered there was a positive, purposefulness to his self-imposed semi-isolation. Parole was only a few months away. He was determined he was going to make it this time. He didn't want anything to go wrong now, like being in the wrong spot when a yard fight broke out.

* * * * * * * * * * * * *
* * * * * * * * * * * * *

I didn't have much of a family. It was just me and my mother. I have a brother and sister at least twenty years older than me, uncles and cousins, but we were never very close. In my family, it was dog eat dog. Everyone looked out for himself. It was nothing like, "If we all pull together, we can make it."

My mother played the major role in my life. She was a Southern woman—from Arkansas. She loved to cook. She was a righteous, God-loving woman. She wasn't too well educated, but she was strong and understanding. I was 13 or 14 before I figured out how she always knew I was the one who had broke something in the house and things like that—Man! I was the only one around!

She sacrificed for me to get an education, never missed my birthday. She raised me on the Golden Rule. I'd never talk back to her. She did what she could for me. I was spoiled.

I never knew my father. I've only seen him twice in my life. The last time was at my high school graduation. I have no regrets about him, no sorrows, no feelings for him. You know what I mean?

* * * * *

I began doing drugs when I was twelve. It was the thing to do. Now, I can see that was the beginning of my life going downhill, but, then, it was the thing to do to be in the "in crowd."

My mother didn't know about the drugs at first. When she found out, she wouldn't allow it in the house. Once in awhile, I'd still do it there, but I'd burn some incense first to hide the smell. One time she found some pot I had. When I came home, she told me she had flushed it down the toilet. I went to my sister's all upset, and she called my mother and told her I owed for that pot, and, if I didn't pay up I'd be in big trouble. She gave it back to me then. She hadn't really flushed it. Eventually, she let me drink beer in the house.

I started selling in the ninth grade. I couldn't live on the two dollars my mother gave me for lunch money. I needed to sell to stay in with the "in crowd," to have money for the things they did. You know what I mean? Selling was my life, my bread and butter. I was a follower. I wasn't thinking ahead. I wanted it all *now*. Man!

I had to be cool and aggressive at the same time. I went to school early to sell, because I had to compete with the real popular guy I sold for. I spruced-up my joints to make them look bigger. I would sell out about 10:30 a.m., and when it was gone, so was I. I'd go to my sister's and get high. She was hip. I sold until I was twenty-six. I became "the Man." You know what I mean? Everybody came to me for drugs.

I was shot twice; once when I was sixteen, and again, when I was a senior. It wasn't gang related, as such, but was over control of the street sales. I've put gasoline in light bulbs, thrown the gas bombs through the front door, and popped them as they ran out the back, and things like that. I'm not proud of that, but, Man, it was part of the street life I was in—dog eat dog. But now I've been there, done that.

I never got caught with dope. I kept it low key. The first rule is: if you don't know them, you don't sell to them. I couldn't believe all the people I met out here in California who were in prison for selling to cops. That's stupid.

Sometimes I'd go to a friend's house. His mom bootlegged liquor. I started drinking. I had a job selling snow cones from a truck, but I lost it because of drinking.

My grades were mostly C's. I was doped up all the time at school. I got up in the morning, drank a beer, smoked a joint, and I was ready for school.

When I was a junior, I got arrested for armed robbery. I was sent to a halfway house, and got caught up on my credits there. In my last year, I had three P.E. classes. I graduated in 1979.

At one time, I was the star free styler on the swim team, and I ran the 100-yard dash in 10 seconds flat! Man! I used to dream of playing professional basketball, but sex, drugs, and rock 'n roll took care of that. Drugs and money overruled all my dreams. To me, loaning, selling, collecting was like a job. It was my life.

* * * * *

I fathered my first child when I was thirteen. It was aborted. When I was 17, I had a son. He's about nineteen now. I've only seen him four or five times. I didn't think he was mine, and I caught a social disease from her, but he looked just like me, so that raised a doubt. We were never close. You know what I mean?

My third child was a girl. We were very close. She lived with her mother, but I helped support her. She used to call me, "Sir Papa Cool." She was killed last year—shot five times. She was only seventeen. I found out from a letter I got here in prison. That hurt me real bad, Man. I cried. There was no one to talk to. There are very few people in prison you can talk to about things that hurt you. It's seen as weakness, and it's used against you. I wasn't there for her like I should have been. Now I have no reason to go back to St. Louis.

I'm supposed to have another one out there. She has my last name. I've seen her two or three times. She is about six or seven now, I don't know, I'm ashamed to say.

* * * * *

I joined the Navy when I was twenty. I failed the test twice before passing. My brother had been in and he made it sound pretty good. I did some checking and the Navy paid a little more than the others, so I chose it for the money, and to be "a man," you know what I mean? Somehow, ideas about college got sidetracked.

I'd never been out of St. Louis before, and didn't know the ways of the world. I only knew the ways of the streets. I was spoiled, had a negative attitude, and was still drinking. I only stayed a year.

My first day at base after boot camp, my room was searched. They found reefer seeds that weren't mine. I was cited for it and my chances for school were taken away. I was angry and felt there wasn't any justice.

Then I got sent to a ship and was making $1,000 a month. I thought, "Hey, Man, this isn't so bad!" But I got expelled for hitting an officer.

* * * * *

When I came back to St. Louis, I started attending nursing school. My mother was in the hospital with cancer. I went to see her twice a day, before and after school. The last thing she said to me was, "Finish school." The next morning she couldn't talk, and after school she was dead. That's the only time I've thought about suicide. She was the love of my life.

My mother left me her house. I let my sister and her boyfriend move in, but that didn't work out. They took advantage of me, and took my money, so I had to kick them out.

My uncle gave me a minimum wage job, but I couldn't pay my bills and take care of my daughter on it. I finished school, but couldn't find a job.

My mother was the only person I had who I could really count on. She kept me balanced and trying to better myself. When she died, I was all torn up. I went off the deep end. I went back to the old crowd and started selling PCP. My drug partner from high school was still selling. He had a wife, house, car, money—I wanted a piece of that, too.

I was fucking like crazy, had a car, and was dressed to impress. I sold from the house. That went on for about four years, until one night I was out cruising around, dressed to impress, and I stopped at a drugstore everyone went to. One of the clerks—a friend of my mother's—looked at me with disgust and said, "If your mother could see you now, she'd turn over in her grave!" I knew she was right, and I started crying.

*   *   *   *   *

I sold the house, moved to California and lived with my brother. I wanted to get a new start. I was twenty-six then. I got jobs as a nurse and flipping hamburgers. Things were looking up.

I went to prison in 1990 because of a white friend. We did all kinds of things together. He came to my place, I went to his. But when he was with his white friends, he didn't know me. One night he called me "nigger," and that led to assault. I felt belittled—like a piece of shit. I went at him feeling, *"You're going to know me when I'm through!"* That led to three years at level one.[6]

I didn't get into the colors.[7] I mixed with both Crips and Bloods. When things came up, I didn't get involved with the gang things, just with those dealing with my friends.

---

6. The lowest of the four securing levels in the California prison system.

I learned self-control inside. I told myself, *"If you can make it in here, you can make it on the outside."*

When I got out, I was still trying to be cool. I wasn't trying to succeed or to apply myself to my capabilities. After thirteen months, I went back on a parole violation for another ten months. That's when I found out I had a little girl.

I was out ten days, then back again. It's been back and forth ever since.

* * * * *

I parole in three months, and I'm changing now. I've lost everything abusing myself and missing good opportunities. Prison has given me time to think about what I should be doing. I've made decisions about what to do with my life. I've mellowed out, lost my vindictiveness. I'm squaring-out.

Since I've changed my attitudes toward life, things have started changing for me. The Lord has helped me with situations. I can see he has helped me overcome problems inside and outside. As long as I'm doing the right thing, I know the Lord is working with me. I need to be patient.

If I live my life with righteousness, it should work this time. I've already done money, guns, knives—you know what I mean? I'm through with that. What did it get me?

---

7. Street / prison gangs adopt colors for gang identification.

There has to be a reason for what happened to me. I'm part of the problem. My past life came from drugs. I kept getting high, living the street life, being cool. I had some good jobs, but I couldn't keep them because of drugs. Nothing changed in twenty-four years! The last sixteen years of my life have been stupidity! It's been a waste of my life.

Now I'm thirty-six. I've got a life of my own. I don't want to go back to the people who helped me get here. I don't need those guys. When you need a favor, they aren't there; they don't remember what you've done for them. I'm tired of hanging out with people who are up to no good, who aren't going nowhere. There is no real belonging, no loyalty.

I've made decisions inside me, and I don't want to come back. Nine years is enough. I'm not super-intelligent, but I'm not dumb either. I'm going to do it the right way this time. Hard work will pay off—people will notice. I'm not ashamed to flip burgers again, or to do odd jobs.

The only obedience I knew was to my mother and to the dope game. They were my whole world. I didn't understand that the way I committed to them was what was needed for a job and the whole of life.

* * * * *

What do I regret? I have too many regrets. I haven't applied myself, or lived up to my potential for anything worthwhile. I wasn't there for my daughter. I didn't go to college. I had all the priorities wrong.

You know, maybe I don't have any regrets. We should learn from our mistakes. The way I am now is from learning from all that has happened to me.

I grew up Baptist, sang in the choir. I rarely pray; sometimes *"Thank you"* or *"Help me."* He knows what is going on, there's no need to go sobbing to him. I believe in Murphy's Law—you know, *"Whatever could go wrong will"*—It's up to the person to overcome them by doing right things. There will always be setbacks, but eventually things go right.

I want a hand up, not a handout. There are organizations out there that can help me get started. I may have to use social services. I'm going to make the system help me. I won't have time to hang out; I'm going to be trying too hard, working too hard. I'm tired of living like this, and I intend to put an end to this shit.

* * * * *

My fears? Myself.. I'm afraid of the damage I could do to myself and others. Look at my scars—my tattoos of life. I don't need anybody drawing things on me. All these came from the color green.

* * * * *

Five years from now, I'd like to have a place, a car, my daughter with me, a bank account, a job—not from the street, but from hard work. I want to find a church.

I'm going to take it one day at a time. I don't want to put a lot of pressure on myself to get a house and things like that, because that's what makes it easy to do the wrong things to get them. I did a robbery once to get $50 I needed, when I already arranged for a loan the next day!

I have dreams, though. Number one is to stay out of prison and to get off parole—to walk on the straight line. You know what I mean? No more riffraff. I want to find my daughter and do right by her, to give her the guidance to live right, and to make her happy. Getting ready to start on these things is what is keeping me going right now.

* * * * *

I don't have anybody out there. I wish I had that—eventually I can get that. I'm not worried about that; I'm used to it. Whatever is going to happen, I have to do it myself. I'm starting over from scratch.

I don't know where my brother is. I haven't heard from him in two years. I'm looking forward to checking-in on my daughter. That's one positive thing to help keep me on track and away from the bullshit.

I haven't met a truthful person yet in California, who has called me "friend" and had honor, who didn't try to manipulate me somehow. A real friend is like a marriage—if you have one, you can count on him. There is no reason to lie. When I say something, it happens. If I have something you need, I give it. But, if you cross me once, there is no second chance.

I want someone to love me for me. I never had that, except for my mother. I'll find someone who will love me as I am, because when I leave I'm not going to have my head up my ass.

Am I going to make it? I'm going to knock them out, Man! You know what I mean?

* * * * * * * * * * * *
* * * * * * * * * * * *

A few weeks before his parole date, Lewis was notified he was being transferred the next day to another prison, and to turn in all of his personal belongings. This unexpected and—as with everything in prison—unexplained change in his plans, really upset him. He set about both getting ready to leave, and trying to find a way to be scratched from the bus list.

Without time to prepare anything, but not wanting him to leave without some kind of sendoff, I quickly organized a going away party with his weight lifting partner, another friend, Lewis and myself. We met that night in the bleachers. I provided ice cream and sodas.

Initially, the conversation was light and vacuous, the kind of shallow bantering men who really care about each other often do when feeling close, but not knowing how to show it. I could sense it would go on that way, and end abruptly without closure when yard recall was announced. I decided to risk trying to bring things to a different level. *"Well, guys, you know Lewis is leaving us tomorrow, and I thought it would be nice to send him off with a prayer."* At that, I reached out with both hands, and, to my relieved surprise, we immediately had a full circle of clasped hands.

I began a prayer asking God's blessings on Lewis as he prepared to parole, for fulfillment of his good intentions and hopes for his future life, and offering thanks for the friendships we had shared. When I ended, I expected silence to set in, but, to my delight, each of his friends joined in with a beautiful, personal sharing, followed by Lewis. Lewis' prayer was hopelessly flawed from a liturgical perspective, but was moving in its heartfelt sincerity. He let us know how much we had touched him and how much it meant that we cared enough to gather with him. All of us were affected by the unexpected emotional sharing we had spontaneously allowed to happen.

As we went back to our cells, I offered another prayer of thanks to God for what we had shared. It was a rare moment of simple, genuine, unguarded humanity. It was something that might have been taken for granted elsewhere, in most other going away parties, but was felt in us as dew on parched land. It was a turning point, and our prayers were answered beyond our expectations.

After a rushed farewell in the morning, which included promises to keep in touch, and an awkward hug, I left for work. All day, I felt bad that I hadn't felt free enough to express the affection I felt for him more directly. It seemed like daylight had exposed our discomfort at having been emotionally "naked" together the night before. That, plus, the close proximity of the other, brought out that debilitating fear of demonstrative affection, which makes emotional cripples of many men.

Returning home from work, I was greeted by Lewis! He didn't know why, but he had been dropped from the bus list. He ended up staying until he paroled. Those few last weeks were the fertile soil in which the seeds of openness, affection and friendship could set root, and practice blossoming.

During those days, we talked, walked, joked and went to meals together. Arms around each other was both common and comfortable. Two very different people, with very different backgrounds, and, in many ways, with very little in common, yet we shared a mutual affection. One night, Lewis came to my door and gave me a card he had paid someone to make. In it he said, *"You are like a father to me—the father I never had and I love you."* He didn't know what to do or say, something like an adolescent at the door on his first date. Expressing sentiment was still foreign to him.

Risking vulnerability and rejection had not been easy walls to breach. For my part, I had struggled all my life trying to learn how to integrate intimacy into my own relationships with family and friendships. More often than not, I left others hurting and wanting. I realized almost instantaneously that I had allowed Lewis into my heart in a way for which I was now responsible. Knowing his story— the painful loss of his mother ("his one love"), and the betrayal of his white "friend" (the hurt of which had led to the assault conviction from which he was now about to parole)—I knew I had become accountable for the love and trust Lewis was risking to place in me. I understood the truth of the fox's admonishment to the Little Prince who had domesticated him, and who had just announced he was leaving—*"You are responsible for what you have tamed!"*[8] I stepped into the hall and gave Lewis a big hug. I didn't care who might be watching, or what they were thinking.

✳ ✳ ✳ ✳ ✳

In the remaining days before Lewis left, I tried to get him to plan his approaching freedom, and to articulate the steps needed to accomplish that plan. His head and heart were ready to do it "right" this time, and to start a new life, but it was difficult for him to be specific about anything, or to project himself into a world and lifestyle that—I realize now—he had never really experienced.

Lewis left prison in mid-November 1997 with the clothes he was wearing and the $200 given to all prisoners as they walk out the gate. In Lewis' case, he had to report to his parole officer in eastern Los Angeles County the next day. He had no one waiting for him, no place to live, no

---

8. Antoine de Saint-Exupery, *The Little Prince* (Harcourt Brace & Co., 1968).

job. When he arrived, his gate money had been diminished by Greyhound fare, first night's lodging and meals.

His parole officer referred him to a boarding house that took in men with drug and alcohol-problem backgrounds. He shared a room with three other men, and had use of a common kitchen for $200 a month. He signed up for general relief assistance the same day. With luck, he could count on his first $214 monthly check in the last week of December—five weeks later.

Like so many others leaving prison in similar circumstances, Lewis had about as much chance of making it on his own, as a pet canary set "free" in a forest. As one of the other men put it, *"The scariest thing is to walk out of here and not have anywhere to go, or anyone to go to, and that's the way it is for 80% of the guys. A lot of their families have given up on them, or are ashamed of them—'What are we going to tell our friends? Oh, he's out of state, up in Alaska.'"*

I had anticipated the impossible situation in which he would find himself, and had given him the phone numbers of a friend in a nearby city, and my brother and sister-in-law. I had already shared Lewis' situation with them, and had received a willingness to be supportive during the crucial first weeks of transition.

Lewis soon made contact with both resources, and received financial assistance, and practical advice regarding job-hunting, enrolling in school, and such. Perhaps, just as important to his well-being, was that he had people to phone and write. While I suffer for many of my companions who have no one to call, and who received no mail and visits, I have no experience of what it feels like not to have someone to answer your calls or to write—people, who through those simple, everyday rituals, give affirmation of another's very existence.

Within two weeks, I received the first of almost weekly letters. Lewis was feeling positive and hopeful. He liked where he lived, had started attending 12-Step groups, was giving talks about drugs to youth groups, and had taken the entrance placement tests for the local junior college. He was happy and off to a good start! After a month, I received a photo of him standing proudly with his arms crossed, wearing sunglasses, and sporting new clothes. His grin was full.

On my part, I wrote back every week to let him know he was still very much in my heart and prayers. We both expressed more easily our closeness in writing, than we had done in person. He wrote to his other friends, too. The "old timers" assured me that his letters were signs that he was moving in the right direction. (Those who are returning to the dead-end lifestyles that brought them to prison don't write.)

Happily, Lewis was able to reconnect with his seven-year-old daughter, Amy. He sent a photo of the two of them, each obviously grateful to be with the other. His letters radiated his happiness and hope: *"This is the first time in a while that I feel worth anything"…"This is the first time I do feel loved, and that I love myself"…"You bring out the best in me, and I'm going to do my best to keep you proud of me."* A short time later, Lewis was diagnosed with both HIV and hepatitis C.

✳ ✳ ✳ ✳ ✳

Within four months, the initial "glow" was dimming, and the struggles of adjusting to "reality" were setting in. Lewis had received a tuition grant, and had enrolled in remedial English and math, and a P.E. class at the junior college. Learning how to learn again was harder than anticipated, and he soon found himself floundering. He panicked and reverted to the familiar coping escape of drugs. As a result, he was kicked out of his boarding house.

My concern grew, as Lewis wandered for a month. Each letter came from a different address. My attempts to communicate words of encouragement, challenge and practical advice, were frustrated by the time lapse between his letters and my responses (due to prison inspection processing). My letters were all returned as *"Not At This Address— Unable to Forward."*

Lewis was obviously very confused, scared, depressed and feeling very much alone. He wrote: *"I think it's just the pressure coming down on me. I really can't think straight. It's not the drugs, I am just feeling down about this school thing that I can't get it together, and I don't understand what is going on! I am just feeling too much. You know, sometimes I feel I'd be better off back in prison. At least I knew what to do there! Is this one of the obstacles you used to talk about?"*

Finally, a letter came from his new apartment. In it, he said, *"If I told you everything was OK, it would be a lie, but things are better and I'm trying hard again."* I was greatly relieved! Lewis had survived his first serious bout between his dreams for a new life, and the inner demons from his past life. But I knew this was just "round one."

* * * * *

After three months of hand-to-mouth struggling, and of good intentions unable to set root, Lewis disappeared again. At the end of October 1998, I received a letter: *"I know you are worrying about me not writing you, but the reality is that I wanted to give up on myself, so I went out! But then I read your last letter again and asked myself what would you do? So I did what was right and checked into a medical treatment center."*

By his first anniversary as a "free" man, Lewis was beginning his third start, again with nothing, since everything he managed to gather each time disappeared with each fall. This time, he and a "lady friend" shared an apartment. He knew there was no love, and that he was making a mistake, but he was lonely and couldn't afford even a cheap apartment on his own. By the time he was arrested in March for assaulting her, he knew for sure.

From the Los Angeles County Jail, Lewis wrote that he was attending a Bible study and an anger management class, and that he was feeling at peace again. *"I feel blessed by your love, the only person on earth who cares a damn for me!"*

* * * * *

The return to prison ended his contacts with Amy. He was not even able to salvage a photo of her. Now at San Quentin, with a release date of April 2001, Lewis still pursues his spiritual growth. *"I really sat myself down this time and figured out what I was missing in my life, and that was God! All that running and not having anyone to trust in life made me a different man. I am coming together today."*

Lewis hasn't mentioned what comes next, when he leaves the security and structure of prison as a "free" man once more. He will have $200 and a Greyhound ticket to…where?

* * * * * * * * * * * * *
* * * * * * * * * * * * *

What private corporation could consistently produce a 67-75% failure rate[9] in its products without a stockholder revolt? California

---

9. 1996 figure taken from a Legislative Analyst's Office report, *Reforms for Parole System Urged*, The Sacramento Bee, 19 Feb. 1998.

taxpayers need to know that their prison and parole systems are failures. The system's "graduates" return to the streets without the social or economic skills, or the transitional support to make it. The system presumes they will fail, sets them up for failure, then punishes them again for failing.

California's Little Hoover Commission's (studies state government and agencies) January 1998 *Report on Corrections in California* soberly and succinctly portrays the system as dysfunctional and failing. Regarding parole it says in part:

> "The statistics illustrate that locking up criminals is only half the job of protecting public safety. The other half is taking advantage of the time prisoners spend in state custody—in prison and on parole—to prepare them to function as responsible citizens, prevent them from committing future crimes and cycling back into prison."

> "...the failure of parolees to reintegrate into society exacts another cost: more crimes and more victims, demonstrating that public safety is ill served by a corrections strategy that only protects the public when the inmate is in custody and does not prepare the inmate to be a responsible citizen..."[10]

* * * * *

---

10 *Beyond Bars*, The Little Hoover Commission Report on Corrections in California, Jan. 1998:46,4 (see Resources).

"The legislative analyst recently documented the dangerous and expensive failure of the state's parole system. The governor and legislators need to pay attention. Both public safety and public dollars are at stake.

"California taxpayers spend $245 million a year to monitor 100,000 newly released inmates. An astounding 67 percent of them return to prison because they fail on the streets, either by committing new crimes or by violating the conditions of their parole. That's a higher parolee failure rate than in any other state. When parolees fail, taxpayers spend another $1.5 billion to return them to prison and maintain them there.

"It's money that would be better spent, as the analyst recommends, on housing, drug and alcohol counseling and job help, programs to assist ex-cons, many of whom are mentally and socially fragile, to live productive, crime-free lives.

"Sadly, California invests almost nothing to reduce parolee failure....Some 80,000 parolees are unemployed, but the parole system offers no job help for most of them; 85,000 are alcoholics or drug addicts, but the system has only 750 treatment beds; an estimated 10,000 are homeless, but there's shelter space for just 200....

"No doubt the legislative analyst's report will be dismissed by some as a liberal, soft-on-crime document. It is not. Money spent to help former criminals conquer their drug and alcohol addictions, get jobs and lead stable lives is cost-effective crime prevention."

(Editorial, The Sacramento Bee, 23 Feb. 1998.)

Armando—"Different From Now On!"

Armando is a contrast of sight and sound. He is tall, handsome and athletic. He walks quickly with a springing energy. Everything about him communicates deep intensity and power. He rarely smiles or laughs, but, when he does, his dark brown eyes sparkle, and the crow's feet at their outside edges create the effect of aged wisdom. Listening to him, it quickly becomes evident that what he has learned has come the hard way and on the streets.

His jet-black hair sweeps back to his neck, where the first tattoos appear. They cover his arms, legs and torso, and tell the story of his life prior to 1993: the Grim Reaper with his scythe (symbol of the The Hoods, his Santa Barbara street gang); and, identifying himself as a "Southerner,"[11] "SUR" (Southern United Raza), "13" and "Sureño." Among the others are a man with a gun and "211" (California Penal Code for armed robbery), and a tower representing prison—Armando's home for nineteen "wasted" years of his life.

All this belies the deep spiritual conversion which has totally turned around Armando's heart, life and life direction, but, nonetheless, remains permanently etched as an unneeded reminder of the "wasted years."

Armando's story is one of pain—both felt and inflicted—and redemption; of great personal courage, amazing grace, and new beginnings. He paroled to a loving wife and teenage son, and, at 35, had dreams and determination for a new life.

---

11. Prison and street Mexican gangs divide against themselves — North and South — using Bakersfield as their arbitrary border.

But it wasn't always that way.

∗   ∗   ∗   ∗   ∗

Two themes that return as refrains throughout Armando's story are the pain of emotional abandonment by his mother, and the sense of himself as "predestined" to be bad. The former seems to have fed into the other. I wondered if not having had the succor of his mother in his loneliness and fears, had not somehow been transferred and let out in his unfeeling and uncaring in regards the fear and pain of his victims.

The internal questioning of his mother and her failures to mother him, occupies a great deal of Armando's memories and reflections. When he vents his questions and feelings related to her, it is with more anger than pain. He doesn't understand how she could be as she was. It is as though he knows so clearly what his mother should have been, that it must have been obvious to her, as well. And, that being the case, why wasn't she what he needed her to be?

His questioning of why he turned out "bad" is not blamed on his mother (although he wonders if he would have turned out differently, had she been different?). He accepts responsibility for his choices and actions. At the same time, it is as if, from his earliest years, he was handed a script and given the role of being the family's scapegoat, the one chosen to actualize its "shadow side." It isn't that he feels he didn't have a choice, or that "the devil made me do it," but that he feels he just turned out the way he was *meant* to be.

As I listened to Armando talk about his gang involvement and his crimes, I was struck by his detachment from both. While the gang gave him a place to belong, and there was a mutual loyalty shared, in a deep personal sense, *Armando* was not there. It was as if he were reading from a script that he had acted out with other actors. There was no emotional bond to the others, no inner purpose being served by the crimes committed, no identification with the persons being injured. I kept watching, as he recounted his stories, for some sign of any feelings that the remembering disturbed him, but he seemed devoid of feelings as he spoke.

*   *   *   *   *

Every time Armando talked about a job he had held, his voice and demeanor changed. He found self-worth in his work, and took pride in being a good worker. His jobs seemed to give him glimpses of his identity and purpose, something that allowed him to demonstrate to himself and others that he could be more than he was. The feedback he received from his employers was that he was good and valued.

As with his work experiences, through encounters with religious people, the clouds occasionally parted to give Armando glimpses of who and what he could be. Each contact touched something in him and left a seed for a future harvest. But, for much of his life, there was too little to nurture his spirit, and too much that was diametrically opposed.

Armando's stoic, hardened features soften, and his eyes glisten, when he speaks of his son and wife. He seems to inherit his soul when he is with them—in person, memory or imagination. He is keenly aware of how his absence brought so much pain into his son's life, and he radiates when speaking of his wife. He has difficulty believing that she can love him as she does. Her faith in God and her faith in him gradually became the bridge over which he became able to cross from one life to another.

*   *   *   *   *   *   *   *   *   *   *   *
*   *   *   *   *   *   *   *   *   *   *   *

My father died when my mom was six-months pregnant with me. My mother married again, and we've lived all of our lives in Santa Barbara. I'm in the middle of two brothers and two sisters.

I was the black sheep of the family. I have a cousin, who is one of ten children, who is the only one in his family who has been in trouble. It was kind of accepted that every family has one. I was ours.

I look back, and I blame my parents a lot, but it's *me* who turned out like this. I ask myself, *"Why didn't my brothers and sisters turn out like me?"* They were raised in the same house by the same parents, and none of them ever got in trouble with the law. All of them finished high school, and have good jobs.

I've tried to look back and figure out why I ended up as I did. Was it my upbringing—the way I was raised? Was it the things I've seen and experienced? It just seems I went the way I was supposed to go. It was the thing to do. It was natural.

I don't remember too many good times as a child, as far as happiness goes. I don't remember birthdays or Christmases. I think my mother was struggling financially. When I was 4 or 5, I remember my brother and I went into a neighbor's house and took some toys.

I've always been afraid of the dark. I remember being locked in a room when I was 4 or 5. I was the only one in the room. It was dark, and I was yelling and screaming. Just the other night, I remembered that, and I was wondering, *"Why was I locked in and left afraid?"* I must have done something wrong.

When I was about 10, my mother, stepfather and uncle started being coyotes.[12] We went to San Diego in a 14' van, and stayed in hotels and ate in restaurants. We brought the illegals to Santa Barbara and kept them in my stepfather's brother's shop.

We started having birthdays and Christmases after that, and my mom bought us things. There wasn't any real excitement or joy in life, though.

* * * * *

I was the only one of the kids who was never disciplined. The others were. At night, when it was time to go to bed for school, my mother would call all the others in. She'd call their names, but not mine. I was always the last kid in the neighborhood to go home. I had to knock on the door to get in, and my brother would get up and let me in.

My mother made sure everyone else was in and okay, except me. When I think about it now, it upsets me. Didn't she care? Did she feel sorry for me because of my dad? I think about these things now, when I'm in bed.

* * * * *

I was never very good in school. I got D's and F's—every once in awhile a C-. I was always fighting and getting suspended. But, I was great at track: 100 yard dash, the 220, 440 relay, high jump, pole vault. I did it in 8th and 9th grades. I really enjoyed it.

---

12 Term used for those who smuggle illegal aliens across the Mexican border.

No one from my family ever came to my track meets. The coaches were only interested in winning and being the number-one school. I think now, if someone had encouraged me, or given me some praise—"*Good job, Armando!*"—I may have had the motivation to build my life around it. But, as I began my negative lifestyle, I gave it up.

I started drinking in the 8th grade. The older boys I hung around with would give me beer. We'd go down to the park and drink. It was a good feeling getting on a buzz.

That was the time of my first trouble with the law, too. After school one day, a friend and a girl broke into the metal shop with me. No one liked the teacher, and he had this fancy chess set he had made which he really prized, so we took it and a few other things.

My friends told on me, though. I was taken to the principal's office. My mother, the teacher and an officer were there. I was told what I'd done was burglary and I could go to juvenile hall. The teacher said he didn't want to press charges, just to get his chess set back. They told me if I returned it within a half hour, I'd only get a two-week suspension, so I ran and got it.

About that same time, an older cousin and another guy would pick me up at the boys' club, and we'd go to the riviera area, to where the nice houses were. I'd crawl through a window and open the door for them. Then, I'd wait in the car. If anyone came, I'd honk the horn. They gave me $20–30 each time. I thought it was a lot, and I was happy.

* * * * *

I met my son's mother in the 8th grade. A year later, when she was 15, I got her pregnant. She had an abortion.

From the 8th grade on, I really got rebellious. I got arrested for grand theft auto, and got six months in the juvenile hall. That was my first time on probation.

Then I burglarized a jewelry store, and got sent to a boys' camp for a year. I got violated after I got out for assault and battery at a high school football game, and got sent back to camp again.

Soon after I got out the second time, me and my so-called friends were drinking one night. One said, *"Get me that bike in the window, and I'll give you $500."* It was an expensive racing bike, so, with two other friends, I smashed the window of the store, took the bike, and started riding it away. But the police came quick, and I ended up hitting the police car, then taking off running, but I got caught. I was sentenced to the Youth Authority, but I used weight pins to get over the fence at juvenile hall, and got away. From then on, it has been in and out of trouble; in and out of being incarcerated.

When the '77 Continentals came out, I stole one, brought it home, and had it parked in the backyard. My mom saw it, but only said, *"You'd better get it out of here."* It was the same when I brought home guns, TVs or anything. My mother didn't want it around, but I was never disciplined or told what I was doing was wrong. Maybe if I had been disciplined or taught, or, if they had called the cops, I would have turned out different? When I get out, I'm going to confront my mom, and ask her why I never was. I knew what I was doing was wrong, but I didn't care, because I knew I wouldn't get in trouble.

I think about these things a lot now. I have a lot of questions. I ask myself, *"Why didn't anyone in my family tell me to shape up?"* It was like I was supposed to be the way I was.

*   *   *   *   *

When I got out of camp the second time, I got the same girl pregnant again. She was 16 then. We'd gone together since she was 13. Her parents kicked her out, and she moved into our house. We were together only a short time after Vincent's birth, because I was just starting to get into trouble and going down. She finally gave up on me. When Vincent was four, she started going out with a former cop named Tim. She finally married him. I don't have any contact with her now.

Until Vincent was six, I kept in close contact with him whenever I was out, but not at all when I was incarcerated.

* * * * *

I got my first job at a produce place after I left camp. I met the guy from the store at camp. I worked in the kitchen and he delivered the produce. He told me to look him up when I got out. I worked part-time stocking, taking orders and loading trucks.

* * * * *

I was eighteen when I joined the East Side Hoods. I was hanging out and partying with them—there were about eighteen guys—and they asked me if I wanted to be "jumped."[13] So, I joined.

The gang gives you a group you can have confidence in when you need them. If you're having problems on the street with someone, they back you up, and vice versa. Our rivals were in the nearby cities. We'd

---

13. Initiation rite during which the gang beats up the new member for about 3 minutes.

rumble with them when they came to Santa Barbara for dances, cruising and things.

When you are in prison, you are expected to get politically involved with the gang agenda: fighting their battles; dealing with rats, child molesters, Northerners, blacks, gang drop-outs. Membership means making a commitment, and taking on a lot of responsibilities.

* * * * *

When I was 18 or 19, I went to a nightclub with some friends one night. I saw a guy who had snitched on some of our friends, who were in jail then as a result. I pointed him out to one of my friends. He went up to him and called him a rat.[14] He looked over and saw me, and figured I was the one who had told my friend. He came over all riled-up and asked me if I had called him a rat. I said, *"Yes, because that's what you are!"* We got into it, and he pulled a knife on me. His mistake was pulling it and not using it.

I backed off and went outside to my car. I took a tire iron out of the trunk and put it under the car. Then I went back in. He came back at me and started chasing me with the knife. I ran outside, and he followed me, chasing me around the cars. I grabbed the tire iron and broke his arm with it. I was about to hit him on the head when other people started coming out, so I left.

* * * * *

About the same time, I robbed a market. I got a year in the county jail and five more on probation. When I got out, I got a job, through a

---

14. Informant for police or prison officers.

friend, laying carpet. The man who hired me knew my background and was leery, but he hired me anyway. He was a Jehovah's Witness. I took an interest in the work and asked a lot of questions. He could see I was eager to learn, and he started teaching me.

After six months, he bought my tools and took $30 out of each paycheck until they were paid for. He took a liking to me, and, on weekends, I'd go to his home to take inventory and wash the trucks. I got to know his family.

One day, when we were driving, he said he was a Christian. I said, *"Christian? I thought you were a Jehovah's Witness."* He explained the Jehovah's Witnesses, and that a Christian is a person who believes in Jehovah-God and Jesus, as his savior. I started doing Bible studies at his house for an hour on Sundays. He planted the seed for the work of God, but I wasn't ready. I was still drinking and partying. Thirteen years later the seed got watered.

I had gone to catechism when I was 8 or 9 for First Communion, but I don't remember ever going to church as a family, except for baptisms, weddings, and things like that. I really had no sense of God or prayer until 1993.

* * * * *

One day at Corcoran in 1989, my cellie and I were talking. He asked me, *"With all of your time in Y.A., camp, jail, prison, how much of your life have you wasted?"* He figured his at 15 years, and said, *"Man, that's messed up!"* I began thinking about that.

* * * * *

If you read my police reports, then looked at me now, you'd see a totally different man. I'm not the same person I used to be.

The change began in 1992, when I was going down for this term. I was in the county jail waiting to go to trial for robbery and residential burglary. I was expecting to get 19 years. I had just paroled from Soledad at the end of '91, after 6 years. At my first hearing, I went up against the same D.A. When he saw me, he told my P.D. (public defender), "No deals!"

My son was living with his mother and Tim, his stepfather. The sergeant came in and gave me the name and phone number of a woman at social services, and told me to call her. She told me Vincent was in juvenile hall for his protection. I wanted to know what happened, but she said when I came in for court the next day, she'd explain it to me.

When I got there, she came into the room where I was by myself. She said, *"I know you haven't seen your son for quite a few years, but, for the past three years, his stepfather has been physically abusing him. He wants to see you. His aunt and uncle (his mother's brother) are willing to take him, but we need your permission."* She showed me Polaroid photos of him showing his injuries. I just glanced at them and shoved them away. I couldn't stand to look at them. I can't explain the feelings I had.

They brought my son in. I grabbed him and hugged him. We were both crying. I told him it was going to be okay. All the time, I'm in my jail clothes and handcuffs. He was 10 then. I knew if I had been with him this wouldn't have happened.

Then I went into court for the first custody hearing. I sat with my wife, brother, sister and mother. Right in front of us were my son's mother and Tim, and her brother and his wife. I had so much anger in me. I knew if I'd had a shank,[15] I'd have hit (stabbed) him. I easily could have, he was right in front of me. I agreed to give custody to Vincent's aunt and uncle.

When I got back to jail, people asked what happened. I had so much anger and hatred. I told a guy, *"I'm going to hit him! He's right in front of me at court."* I wanted to kill him. The guy told me he could arrange to get a piece[16] for me when I went back to the sub-station on my way to court.

Those were my plans. Somehow it got to the wrong ears, because, on the way to court, this guy and me were taken apart from the others as we got on the bus, and our feet were shackled and our hands cuffed at our waists. When I got to court, I was taken to the opposite side from where Tim was.

After court, the cops took me into this room and told me they had three witnesses who said I was planning something. I told them I didn't know what they were talking about. They said, *"We found a shank."* I said, *"I don't know anything about it. If you're going to charge me with something, then charge me, but then I want a lawyer here. I don't have anything else to say."* They read me my rights, and put me in a special isolation cell. Eventually, they gave up on it.

I was sentenced to 11 years and sent to prison. For the next two years, I had dreams 2–3 times a month of Tim. I saw myself with a shotgun and wearing a ski mask, squatting behind a car in his driveway at night. He'd come outside to put out the garbage, and I'd shoot him. As soon as

---

15. Knife.
16. Another name for a knife.

I'd hear "Boom!," I'd wake up hyperventilating. My cellie would wake up and ask what was wrong. I'd tell him it was asthma.

I told my wife about the dreams. She told me to pray, and that she would pray that God would take them away.

* * * * *

I remember plenty of times I was hurting, but I had no one to go to. I never felt close to anybody until I met my wife. She's the closest person in my life. I always kept my distance from everyone. I never trusted anyone.

My wife is the only one who ever showed me she cared. I met Nicole when she was the godmother of a cousin's son in 1986–87. We went together until we got married in the county jail in 1992. That was before I started changing, but she was already very strong and active spiritually.

We were engaged and planning to get married when I went down for this term. I told her it would be okay to break it off, that I'd understand, and that we could still be friends. So, we've only had weekend visits and the occasional family two-day visits since we've been married.

When I get out, Vincent is coming to live with us. Nicole has done so much for him. They have fun together. She is really special. It's really rare that you'll find a person like her. I believe it is her love of God that shines through her love and compassion.

When Nicole comes to visit, we read the Bible together, and get down on our knees and pray together. She does that every morning before going to work, and, when I get out, I'm going to join her.

I could talk about her for days and days!

* * * * *

The hatred and anger I had for Tim continued as I began to serve my time. There was this guy on the yard, who was always coming up to me telling me he wanted to share Jesus with me. I'd tell him I didn't want to hear it.

One day, he said, *"I'm an observer, and I see you filled with hatred. The Lord has put it in my heart to talk to you. You never smile; you look like a walking time bomb."* I told my cellie what he said to me, and he said, *"You do look like that. Other guys see it, too, and ask me if you're okay."*

He kept coming around, and would say stuff like, *"Jesus loves you!"* I'd tell him I appreciated his concern, but to leave me alone, but he wouldn't. He asked me if I wanted to do Bible study. I got to the point where I just wanted to sock him!

This guy got my name and number, and sent for Set Free Prison Ministries Bible Study. It came in the mail one day. I looked at it and couldn't figure where it came from. It had my name on it, and the letter said, *"We're happy that you are interested…"* and so on. I was tripping! I read through the stuff and set it on my shelf.

The next day, the guy smiles at me like he knows something, and I connected how I got it. I thought, *"You little bastard!"* Then he asked me if I got it. I said, *"What is it going to take for you to get the message?"* But he wanted to talk. I figured, *"Okay, if I listen to his line, then he'll go away."*

He began to give me his testimony about what the Lord had done for him when he got hooked on drugs. He started again with, *"The Lord has put it in my heart to share with you."* I told him, *"Check this out, Man...,"* and I began to tell him about Vincent and his stepfather, and what I was going through because of it. I ended by telling him, *"I've already decided that when I get out I'm going to blast him!"*

I began to think about what that would mean—that I'd never leave prison again. I thought about my wife and that it wouldn't be fair to her. I told her I thought we should get a divorce, since I'd be coming back for life. She started crying and said, *"Don't think like that. God will take care of it."* I thought to myself—but didn't say out loud—*"There you go again with that God stuff!"* I told her, *"I'm just trying to be fair to you, so you won't be waiting for nothing."* Then I said, "You sound like the guy in the yard who's been after me," and I explained about him and the Bible study coming. She said, *"That's God reaching out to you."*

＊ ＊ ＊ ＊ ＊

Time goes by, and Vincent starts coming with Nicole to visit me. I start listening to this guy more and more. In 1993, I finally began doing the reading and study, but only when my cellie was gone, because I didn't want him to know about it. I was afraid he'd see it as a sign of weakness. I'd go awhile, then I'd put it on the shelf and quit. Letters would come saying, *"We haven't heard from you for awhile..."* Then I'd start again, and slowly began to understand what Jesus did for us. When I finished the first course and got my first certificate, I felt really good! This has been going on for a year now, and nobody knows—not even my wife.

I started a study on prayer, and I told God, *"I need you to help me overcome drugs. I can get killed on them in here."* He did.

People would give me $50 papers.[17] I had it coming for going down for the gang—I was a "Sureño". But, when I began to give my life to God, I stopped using it, so I'd sell them for $25. I justified that because I wasn't using it. But, as I got further along, I knew I couldn't be part of contributing to other people's problems, and I stopped accepting them.

When I was at Wasco, my cellie did heroin. One day he came back to the cell after taking a hit, and I watched him. For the first time I saw what it did to people. I began to ask myself, "Is that how you looked and were when you did it?" It made me sick. It changes your whole personality—makes you look stupid and disgusting.

* * * * *

I finally told Nicole that I had been doing the Bible studies. I told her, "I think I know what you've been telling me about now, and I've got certificates to prove it, too!" She said, "What!!!" and started crying. She got so happy, and had the prettiest smile. She told me how proud she was of me. I sent her the certificates to see, but told her to send them back, because I liked looking at them.

Then I started a study on forgiveness. I found things like: "Unless you forgive others, I will not forgive you," and "Forgive, as I've forgiven you." I thought, "There's no way I'm going to forgive Tim!" And, I put the stuff back on the shelf for six months. I lied to my wife that I was still doing it.

After awhile, though, I started feeling something was missing. I was still having those dreams about killing Tim. I got on my knees and

---

17. Heroin fixes with a $5–$10 street value.

prayed, "Will you teach me to forgive Tim? Show me how. Put the forgiveness in my heart that you have for us." I can't explain how, but he did it.

The first time I prayed for Tim, I told God that I forgave him, and asked him to send him someone who would help him come to repentance and salvation. I knew when I did that, that God was working in my life. I shared what had happened with Nicolle, and she cried and was so joyful!

* * * * *

I kept studying—the books kept getting bigger! I was sneaking into the chapel, afraid of being caught by the homeboys and being embarrassed. I lied to the homies to cover going to the chapel. The package arrival list was kept on the wall next to the chapel door, so, when they asked where I was going, I'd say to check the list. Then, when no one was looking, I'd sneak in.

Then I came upon the passage, "*If you deny me, I will deny you.*" Shortly afterwards, the homies caught me coming out of the chapel. At first, I lied and said I had been looking for a praying-hands pattern to copy, but I finally admitted what I was doing. A couple of them said, "*That's okay.*" I asked forgiveness of God for denying him, and promised, "*Starting tomorrow, I'm not going to be ashamed of you anymore. As a matter of fact, I'm going to start taking my big Bible, instead of the little one I've kept hidden in my pocket.*"

At first, when the homeboys asked what was going on with me, I snapped back defensively, "*Got a problem with it!?!*" Gradually, I came to realize I couldn't be a Sureño anymore; I was a "new man in Christ." I started telling people, "I'm not a Sureño, I'm a Christian. I don't want to know what's going on in the yard anymore; I'm not going to be a part of it." So, I stopped kicking with the homeboys.

I prayed, "I want this comfort, peace and love you talk about. I want to experience them, feel them. I need a lot of help to overcome years of bad habits. I'm going to need your strength. I've always felt if I reached toward you, Lord, you'd reach down and pull me up the rest of the way." He has.

*   *   *   *   *

I've made a lot of decisions about what I'm going to do with the rest of my life, and I'm going to stick to them. I've done the ones I can in here, but there are ones I have to make on the outside. It isn't going to be easy, but I'm going to do it.

First, I'm going to get off parole. That means staying away from *all* bad influences. I know who the people are, some are my relatives. I can't have anything to do with my cousins. They are all into drinking and drugs. I've come to hate what drugs do to people, because I've seen what they've done to my life. I don't want to run with people from my past. It isn't that I'm better than they are now, or that I don't care about them, but because I just can't.

I've had hardly any contact with my family for the past six years. I call them. I've received maybe one letter from one of my sisters; nothing from my brothers. I've written them about coming to know the Lord, and how they need to come to know him and accept him into their hearts. I've told them I'm changing my lifestyle, and that I'm not going to be living as before. I know they are saying to themselves, *"Yeah, right. Sounds good, but Armando isn't going to change."*

My family think they know me, but they really, really don't. I was first incarcerated when I was 12 or 13, and, from then on, I've been in and out, in and out. As a person—what I think and what I feel—they don't know me.

My wife goes to family things. Three years ago, someone said to her, *"I'll give you credit for staying with him, but he is going to just keep going back. He always does."* They're in for a rude awakening. I'm not the same man as six years ago. I haven't changed a little bit—I've changed *totally!* They're going to say, *"Hey, wait a minute, this is Armando, but not the one I know!"*

My younger brother told me on the phone that he had seen Tim, and that he felt like "beating his ass." I told him that won't help. What is done, is done, and all that we can do now is pray for him. He said, *"Wait a minute! That's your son—your flesh and blood!"* I'm not the Armando they think they know.

When my son came to visit the last time, he said, *"Dad, they're planning a big barbecue for you when you get out."* I told him to tell them I won't be there. I didn't see it before, when they threw the parties for me when I got out, but someone would always hand me a beer, then someone else would slip me some drugs. I don't want any of that anymore. I don't want to be around people like that.

In 1988, I was hooked on cocaine. My relatives saw me and knew it. If they really cared, they would have tried to help. But, they saw me all strung out and said, *"If you ever come across a color TV, or a cam-recorder, bring it to me".* I did that one night. I used a brick to break the store window, and took some cam-recorders to my cousin at 2:00 a.m. She gave me $400 then, and told me to meet her at the beach the next day for $600 more. She came, gave me the money, said, *"Thank you,"* and was gone. Now I can see what kind of cousins they are. They didn't care if I was sick, or going to go to jail. And they want to give me a barbecue? That's a bunch of crap! What for? Why should I go? To hear a bunch of lies?

When I was 23, I was really getting bad. I went into my mother's room. I was crying. I said, *"Mom, I need to talk to you."* She said, "What's wrong?" I told her, *"I've got a problem. I'm sick. I slam.*[18] *I need help!"* She saw my arms, and all she said was, *"Why do you do that to yourself?"*

I wanted her to hold me. I had hoped she'd show more concern—try to get me into a program. But there was nothing. That was the first and last time I ever did that! That was it! I left.

Now, I think about it and I get angry. I've always taken the consequences of my actions—I've even taken the fall for my so-called friends. I know I'm responsible for my choices, but I also know my parents didn't fulfill their responsibilities to me. If my son came to me with a problem like that, I'd really try to help. I'd feel, *"That's my son! You've got to be there for him."*

I'm going to be a stranger to my family. They want to give me a welcoming hug and kiss, and tell me, *"We've missed you so much!"* If they missed me so much, why didn't they bother spending 32 cents to write, or to send me a birthday card, or a Christmas card, or stop by to ask Nicole how I was doing?

* * * * *

---

18. Inject heroin by syringe.

I'm going to get my G.E.D. I should have done it while I was here. Then I'm going to take night classes at the junior college.

I'm 85% sure of getting a job laying carpet again with the company I used to work for. I was always a good worker, a damn good employee. I really enjoyed carpet laying. I took pride when I saw the people's faces when they saw the work I had done for them. It feels really good knowing you are good at what you do. It was always the drugs, drinking and partying that blew my jobs before.

*   *   *   *   *

I know what I have to do to be the father I want to be for my son. I can't make up for the other years, but I can do it right from now on. The same for Nicole.

Last weekend, my son was here. He had been in some trouble, and we talked. He had gone to the mall with his cousin, and a couple of guys he didn't know started giving him a bad time for supposedly looking at the girlfriend of one of them. It ended up with them going to the parking lot and fighting. Vincent tried to stay out of it, and told the guys, *"Look, I don't want any trouble,"* and that they were mistaken, but they wanted to impress the girl, so they kept pushing it.

I told him it's okay to defend yourself, but only after everything else fails. It is okay to walk away from a fight if you can. I don't want him to follow in my path.

Vincent is sixteen now. He told me he had good grades. I hugged him and kissed him, and told him how proud I was of him. When Nicolle and I pray, we always join hands. Vincent used to be uncomfortable— would look around to see if anyone was watching. I told him, *"We aren't doing this to impress people, and there is no reason to be embarrassed when we show our respect for God, and our love as a family."*

In the past, after work, I used to go out drinking. Now, I'm going to come home and be what a husband and father should be. I'm going to help Nicole in the kitchen; we enjoy cooking together. We are going to have dinner together as a family, and are going to read the Bible together. I'm going to help Vincent with schoolwork, take walks with him, guide him. Nicole is getting some mountain bikes for us, so we can all take rides, go on picnics. Vincent has never played baseball, so I'm going to get some mitts, so we can play catch. Things like that.

* * * * *

There is something else I want to do. I have a dream. I've had it a hundred times since 1993. I want to volunteer to help the homeless and people like that. In this dream, I see myself going into a market and buying submarine sandwiches, chips, fruit and sodas. I take them back behind the railroad tracks into the bushes where the homeless hide. I feed them, and share the Word with them.

There is another version. It is winter, and I go into the surplus store and buy mittens, sweatshirts, and things. Then I take them to the people.

It's not just a dream either. I *know* I'm going to do it. I've been there, and I know what it is like to be hungry and cold, and not have any place to go, no one to listen to me, no one to share with, or care.

* * * * *

I feel bad when I think about the people I've hurt; the fear I've put in them. I never used to care if I hurt people physically or emotionally. I didn't think about it. It didn't bother me. But, when I hung out with the wrong people and was on drugs, I became a real monster, a real monster.

What keeps so many guys coming back is that they are locked into a self-defeating cycle. They have low self-esteem and see themselves as losers. They see themselves as locked-in, just like I used to think I was supposed to be that way—the black sheep. They don't have any hope that things can be different.

The Department of Corrections? That's a joke. Nothing ever came to me that was good here, except that being here kept me from getting to Tim when I wanted to kill him, and it was the place where I came to know the Lord. I don't know if that would have happened anyway, but it has changed my life and given me another chance.

I don't know why I'm not dead right now. The situations I've been in—I could easily be dead right now.

It's going to be different from now on. Man, are they in for a surprise!

* * * * * * * * * * * * *
* * * * * * * * * * * * *

As Armando's parole date neared, he began getting headaches and losing his appetite. He was consumed with anxiety, and afraid of the "shock" of reentry, after almost ten years of being isolated from making the simplest choices and decisions for himself. He wondered what it would be like to ride in a car again, and to hear one that "talks" to him;

how he would be able to choose from a restaurant menu; whether he could handle the new technology of ATMs, phones and VCRs. He was afraid his wife and son wouldn't understand his need to slowly acclimatize—*"When I walk the dog, ride my bike, or take out the garbage, those are going to be big things for me!"*

During the last few months, Armando stayed more and more to himself and was rarely in the yard. His fears spilled over into worrying that he might just happen to be walking by a group of men when a fight broke out, and he would get "rolled up"[19] by presumed involvement, and have his parole date postponed. He was "practicing" avoidance of people and situations which could violate his parole and return him to prison in spite of his best efforts to make a new life.

The great fear that oppresses the thoughts and feelings of men preparing to parole is that they won't make it. The anxiety begins to build months ahead of time, and, as the waiting time becomes weeks, sleepless nights and loss of appetite are common. This is especially true in men, who, like Armando, have spent much of their lives in the cycle of "in and out"—mostly in.

Younger men do not exhibit these pre-release symptoms, either because they have no intention of changing their lifestyle when they return to the streets, or because they naively believe they can, just by wishing change to happen.

---

19. Refers to rolling up an inmate's bedroll and personal belongings when he moves from a cell, or when he is taken to "the hole" for disciplinary reasons.

After finishing my interviews with Armando, we would occasionally walk in the evening after dinner, and I'd listen as he expressed his fears, and his determination not to let anyone, including his family, become the intentional or accidental cause of returning him to this world, which he was inalterably set on leaving behind forever. He was obsessed with concern. The statistics support the fear which Armando and the more experienced men exhibit.

Only 15% of those who fail parole do so because they commit new crimes. It is unbelievably easy to violate parole, even while striving 110% to make a new life. All it takes is to come into contact with the police for any reason whatever: a minor traffic violation for which "everyday citizens" would receive a warning; accepting a ride in a car from a friend who, unknown to you, has marijuana in his glove compartment; staying at a relative's home, where a hunting rifle is found in a closet when a random check of where you are and what you are doing is made; having a prescription drug, which you are taking for a medical problem, show up on a random drug test. Or, you could miss a scheduled meeting with your parole officer because your car broke down. There is no appeal of your parole officer's determination that you have violated your parole.

Unlike Lewis, who paroled with only the clothes on his back, to no one waiting, no place to live, and no job, Armando was fortunate to be among the minority who left with not only a strong commitment not to return, but also to a strong support system. His wife has a nice home in a nice neighborhood, and, with her and his son, he has a strong, loving family, with a deeply shared spiritual base. Armando also had a marketable skill and a former employer waiting.

Except for a card his first Christmas out, I have not heard from Armando since he paroled. I am hoping he will be among the 26% who make it. If he does, it will not be because of anything the "corrections" system did to or for him.

Curtis—"I Just Want Someone To Love Me!"

I met Curtis when I was assigned as a clerk in the prison office where he worked. Our desks were in different rooms, but within 50 feet of each other, yet it was at least six months before much more than an exchange of "Good Morning" took place. He came in at a brisk pace, not stopping as he passed. If not greeted, he did not initiate an exchange. He kept to himself. When it was time to leave, he left quickly.

After three months, I was promoted to a job which placed our office doors directly across from each other. The proximity and the more frequent contacts led me to reach out more actively. His response was always polite, but never inviting. Only very slowly did our conversations become more real and comfortable.

One day, Curtis shared with me that the man whose job I had taken (who no longer worked in the office) had sexually harassed him, constantly making comments about how he would like to enjoy him sexually. One of the fundamental "rules" of prison life is that no inmate ever "rats" on another. Problems are dealt with through fight or flight, in one form or another. Curtis handled his problem by withdrawing into himself, and avoiding social contact at the office, except with the few people with whom he had become comfortable.

That sharing was my first insight into one fundamental component of the person Curtis is, that of distrust. Distrust is normative in prison life, and a vital survival tool. But, there was more than that at work in Curtis.

With time, and a purposeful sensitivity on my part, a friendship of sorts developed, and he began to entrust me with bits and pieces of his story, limited at first to his legal situation. I could always feel that I was being kept at "arms length," both physically and psychically. At the same time, he seemed to be reaching out wanting to be embraced somehow—to be known and understood. While listening to this man, I felt I was hearing a scared child.

As he became increasingly more comfortable with me, he would regularly come into my office to share something that had happened. He would watch for my reaction, expecting—or hoping for—affirmation, approval, acceptance. I knew from a few earlier innocent "mistakes" that any reaction on my part that he could interpret as critical or non-accepting would lead to his quick retreat, both within himself and from the room.

One day, I told him about *Wounded Wounders*. His reaction was excited interest, so I asked him if he would like to tell his story for my book. He accepted immediately. Our first session was sitting on the grass on the softball diamond near third base. He was very definite about not wanting to use the bleachers, and just where we would sit. It was more isolated and private there, than in the bleachers. I had a feeling he felt safer on the grass. Later, I discovered that he played third base on the quad softball team.

It is impossible to listen to Curtis without being drawn into his pain, and to not want to take it away somehow. His is a story of abandonment and longing, of running and searching, of escape routes which led to quicksand, and of a justice system gone awry. It is also a story of grace and hope.

To meet Curtis, one would never suspect one was in the presence of a convict serving 50 years-to-life. The stereotype Curtis fits is that of the all-American boy. He is white, blond and blue-eyed—not a tattoo or pierced body part mar his youthful good looks. His smile belies the pain underneath. Even with the slight moustache, at thirty-seven, he could easily pass for a high school student. He is 5'7" and athletically trim, thanks to his one great passion—baseball.

All that is good and beautiful in Curtis shines on the baseball diamond. He is confident in himself, fast, alert, professional looking and acting in his uniform. He encourages the other men, gives a supportive word when a play is missed. He throws himself totally into the game, with both mental fixation, and as he hurls himself face first with abandon toward second base. Here, he knows who he is, he knows he is good. Nothing else matters for nine innings. He is happy!

Even during our first session, it was evident that there was an emotional tug-of-war going on within Curtis. He wanted to tell his story to someone, yet he was afraid of hearing it—feeling it—himself. He knew he needed to let it out, but he was afraid he couldn't handle it.

At first, I was incredulous at his lack of memory about so many early things. Not remembering has been one way he has coped with his pain, including that of having been molested by his brother. That event came back to him only after we had finished our interviews, and I had given him the first draft to proofread. He wrote that line concerning the molestation into the text, and told me how remembering that was a very freeing experience for him. We never discussed it further.

I had noticed that Curtis always kept a fixed physical distance from others, whether standing or sitting at work, and while we sat on the grass for our interviews. There was no touching on his part, and he

reacted in a shunning way when touched by others. The one exception
in which he seemed to feel totally comfortable was holding hands during the prayer circles that 6–7 of us inmates would sometimes share in
the mornings at work. Even then, though, he would make sure to be
next to someone with whom he felt comfortable.

Avoidance of conflict was another obvious pattern. As I pictured
Curtis huddled in the garage listening to his parents fighting, I understood the patterns of avoidance I had noticed at the office. Woven into
that pattern is also a terrible fear of abandonment. The triple dynamic
of not wanting to be caught in the crossfire of anger in others, the fear
of allowing anyone to get too close—physically or emotionally—and
the terror of being left alone by someone for whom he cares, had left
Curtis an emotional paralytic.

Curtis' declaration of not caring anymore, reinforced by his common
reference to his mother as "that woman," is only true in that he wills it to
be true, wishes it were true. Even his enraged renunciation of his
mother *as* his mother is a form of crying out for her embrace. That
rejection, which, more than any other single event, seems to define
Curtis' emotional make up, also is the drive behind his unabashed crav-
ing to be loved.

The one time he came close to finding that love was in his wife. She
took on the role of mother, as well as lover. He even made one last futile
attempt for his mothers' blessing of his marriage—a blessing on him.

We cut short the session in which we talked at length about his
mother. Curtis was losing the battle against tears, and I wasn't far
behind him. I put down my pen and tablet, and we just talked about
how we were feeling. I had only recently begun to work through my

own confused relationship with my mother, and I was responding in my own way and categories to Curtis' hurting and confusion.

A few years ago, Curtis discovered the consolation of faith. He has centered his prison life around the Protestant chapel, where he is involved in a variety of studies and ministries. There is a strong streak of fundamentalism in his religious perspectives, but he struggles to overcome the narrow prejudice he knows he has toward those who are "not saved." This tendency has been noticeably tempered by his ongoing friendships with Catholics. Besides me, he now has three pen pals, a nun in her 80s, a priest classmate of mine, and a married woman in whom he has found a feminine spiritual soul mate.

He finds solace, strength and hope in the message of the Bible, and in the love and embrace of God, as well as a feeling of self-worth and purpose in his chapel leadership roles, and in witnessing and leading Bible studies on the yard. He binds himself "morally" to follow even the silliest of prison rules, and gets confused and discouraged when he encounters imperfections in other chapel leaders. Spiritually, as with most other aspects of himself, Curtis is often a lost, hurting child seeking a home in which he will belong, find approval and be loved, but he has come a long way in allowing God and others to affirm and embrace him.

* * * * * * * * * * * * *
* * * * * * * * * * * * *

I don't have very many memories of my childhood—even of high school. I have difficulty remembering events, names, places—especially the feelings that go with them. What I do remember, though, is negative and painful.

I'm the youngest of four. I have a brother and two sisters. I found my youngest sister, Connie, a year ago, after eleven years. I don't know about the others. She came to see me eight months ago, and we write and talk on the phone.

When I was four or five, my father left home to work in Nevada. My mother met this other guy, and asked us if we wanted her to marry him, or *"Do you want to go find your father?"* All of us wanted to find my dad, and we did. We were together again for a while.

One of my good memories comes from this time. It has to do with baseball, the one thing in my life that has always given me joy and self-esteem; even now. I played Little League, and my family came to watch and cheer. It's the only time I can remember when my family was together that there wasn't arguing.

We moved back to the San Fernando Valley. I can remember the times I'd stand in the garage, huddled-up with my brother and sisters, listening to my parents arguing. It was about this time that my brother molested me. Even now I can't handle being around arguing.

At some point—I was still pretty young—my mother took off. My father tried to take care of us. Connie went with my mother. Sara, my other sister and I stayed with my father until he met another woman and wanted to move in with her. I didn't want to be with that woman, so we began a period of bouncing back and forth between our parents. My brother ran away. Later, one of my sisters did, too.

Eventually, they asked us to choose between them, and we went with our mother. But, one day my father kidnaped Connie and me from school, and we moved north someplace.

* * * * *

I don't remember anything about junior high. I don't know what city it was in, the name of the school, or any of the teachers. All I remember is that I got meal coupons to buy lunch in the cafeteria.

When I started high school, Sara ran away to get married. She wasn't really in love with the guy, but it was a chance to get away. After she left, my father moved to Stockton, so I went to stay with Sara and slept on the couch. When her baby came, the place was too small, and I moved in with a friend and his family. I don't remember a lot about them, but they took me on a vacation with them one time, like I was a part of their family. That really meant a lot to me. I really enjoyed that.

I stayed with them until I graduated. I worked on a paper route, and saved most of my money to send flowers to my mother. I'm told I also wrote to her, but I don't remember that. But there was never any acknowledgment. I never heard from her or saw her. I know my mother hurt me real bad.

I wonder now, *"How did I live?"* I don't recall ever getting a phone call to see how I was doing or any money to help me get things I needed.

While I was there, Sara attempted suicide. I didn't go to be with her. I'm not sure how I even found out. I just knew about it somehow.

I did well in school. I never did any drugs. Every couple of months, I'd have a few beers with some of my friends, but I was really clean-cut. Baseball was my life. I pitched, and the friend I stayed with caught. I was "Mr. Baseball!"

My father came to my graduation, but he left before the ceremony. It was really important to me for him to be there. He said, *"It was cold."* It hurt. After that, he moved to Stockton. I moved out of my friend's house. I've never had contact with that family since.

* * * * *

Not long after graduating in 1980, I moved to Stockton to try to find my father, and discovered he was moving to Alaska. I got a job, and started at the junior college.

Since my father was leaving, and he obviously didn't have me in his plans, there was no real reason for me to stay in Stockton. So, after a few months, I joined the Navy. The recruiter promised I would become an electrician's mate, but, when I got to boot camp at San Diego, I was told my scores weren't high enough and that I would be going to fire fighting.

I didn't like the Navy anyway, so my way of protesting them not fulfilling their promise, was to stop saluting the officers. After four months, they decided they didn't like me either, and I was dismissed with an other than honorable discharge and a R-4 rating. That's their lowest.

* * * * *

1981 was a big year in my life. I was 20 and had just bombed out of the Navy. I found my mother through Sara. She wouldn't allow me to know where she lived, or to come to her home, so we met elsewhere. I wanted to talk about the past, to ask, *"Where were you? What about the flowers? Why no contact?,"* but she wouldn't answer my questions. She said, *"You're living in the past."* There were no signs of affection or caring.

I had thought I was old enough and ready to confront her, but after that meeting, everything fell apart. I gave up. I didn't care anymore.

Did I tell you that when I was in prison in 1990, my mother wrote me to say she hated me? She said it was because I chose to go with my father instead of her. That was from when he kidnaped Connie and me.

I don't want that woman to know how I am. I don't want her to have any satisfaction. I want her to think of what she's done, and to question whether she was the cause of me going to prison for life. I don't think she's given any thought to me, though. If so, why hasn't she reached out—even if only for selfish reasons to satisfy her need to know?

My not wanting that woman to know anything about me is so strong, I almost don't want to relate to my sister, so she'd have no way to find out. I'm sure Connie tells that woman "everything is fine." But it isn't! Connie calls her "an awful, evil woman."

Prison has helped me realize how cold the world is, that no one really cares. Whenever I ask myself, *"Who is there for you?,"* it evokes fear. If I had to turn to anyone for help, I don't think there is anyone there. Who cares if Curtis lives or dies? Connie would be hurt and upset, but she's got her own life; she's not there for me. I know that's the "poor, pity me" part of Curtis.

* * * * *

I met Sharon, my future wife, in 1981. I went to work at Jack-In-The-Box; she was my boss. She thought I was obnoxious at first—you know, I was just out of the Navy. She is a very controlling person, but that suited me just fine. People used to ask how I could take it, but I didn't even see it.

I don't remember ever telling Sharon about my family, but she knew somehow. I took her to meet my mother in 1984. My mother didn't like her. I don't know why I took her. Maybe I was hoping to get her approval.

We lived together for a year before we got married in 1985. We had a beautiful, wonderful relationship. If not for the drugs that began soon afterwards, I'm sure we would still be married. Sharon played all kinds of roles for me: mother, father, wife, protector. She always tried to protect me.

*　*　*　*　*

I got my first drugs from my wife's brother. He gave me some cocaine. I put it in my glove compartment, and it sat there for two weeks. One day, I asked a co-worker if he knew how to do it. He showed me. I don't know why I got started. I don't think I was consciously aware of all of my pain then. I guess I thought it was fun, that it was a glamour drug—you know, what rich people did.

They really didn't do much for me at first. It was a month or two before the next time. My brother-in-law taught me how to smoke cocaine. Once I started that, it really took off. My habit grew, but it was periodic, mostly when I had an opportunity. Sharon didn't know about it at first.

Every time I got in trouble with the law, I was high on drugs. The first time, I drove my company truck with the logos on it—I was working as a water-delivery guy—to the drive-in window of a fast food place, and asked the girl for the money. No gun, no nothing. It wasn't hard to catch me, as you can guess. As soon as I came down, I admitted what I'd done. I didn't try to fight it.

✶ ✶ ✶ ✶ ✶

Next time, I was arrested for possession of $20 worth of rock cocaine. While I was waiting to go to court on that, I was charged with two armed robberies of stores. I had nothing to do with either of them in any way. The first one was quickly dismissed when the clerk told them I wasn't the one.

When the clerk from the other store looked at a photo line-up at the police station, he said I looked like the man. He described me as taller than he was, with long hair and no moustache, and with brown eyes. The officer told him, *"You have the right man."* In court, when I stood next to the clerk, he was a few inches taller, I had short hair and a moustache, and I have blue eyes. When asked how he explained the discrepancies, the clerk said, *"I never said he was the one, only that he looked like him."* The officer testified that my moustache looked like eight days' growth to him. Besides that, none of the fingerprints or palm prints found on the scene of the crime were mine.

The robbery took place eight days earlier on Easter. I had photos taken that day at Sharon's family's dinner, showing me the way I looked that day—with short hair and a moustache—but my new, young public defender didn't introduce them as evidence because he said there was no need, *"It's an open and shut case for us."*

The D.A. was allowed to use my drug possession charge against me, and that seemed to sway any doubts the jury had. Anyhow, I was sentenced to nine years in prison for a crime I didn't do and didn't know anything about.

*　*　*　*　*

That same year, 1989, two months before I was sent to prison, my daughter was born. I'd been given a chance to pour all of the love and affection that I didn't receive into my new baby girl. I thought, *I'll show my parents how to take care of a child!* I got out of prison in 1993, just in time for my daughter's first day of school. I only had a year to spend with her before I was sent here for the rest of my life. The moments I spent with her makes it even more difficult for me to understand how parents could walk out of their child's life and never look back.

*　*　*　*　*

When I got out of prison, I tracked my father down in Alaska. I knew the company he worked for, so I checked the phone books and called several cities until I found him at work. I told him I forgave him and didn't hold him accountable. He cried and told me to go my own way because *"the family is no good."* He wouldn't give me his home phone or address. He was telling me to go away.

He gave me this "fatherly advice," *"Stay off drugs."* After that $26 call, I never have had any contact with him again. I don't know if he is alive or dead. I don't care. I feel the same way about my mother. Maybe they gave me all they had, but it wasn't enough.

*　*　*　*　*

It all started crashing down for good in 1995. I was working for myself as a plumber, and I was into rock cocaine pretty heavy. My in-laws had moved, but hadn't sold their house yet. They gave many of the furnishings to Sharon and me to use, and I bought their snowplow. I had a key to the house because I was keeping up the place for them. I'd use the house to smoke cocaine and get high.

One day, while I was high, I sold the furnishings to get more money for rock cocaine. Then I walked to a nearby store. The cash register was open, so I reached in and took $40 and walked out. I was so out of it, I didn't even run, so it didn't take much to catch me. As always, once I sobered up, I admitted what I had done.

My in-laws were furious, and, instead of backing me, they lied and said I had stolen the furnishings and snow plow, even though I had the cashed check for the plow.

I felt so bad about what I'd done and how it was affecting Sharon and my daughter, I agreed to a plea bargain that would keep Sharon from having to testify against her parents or me. I'd already put her through enough, and I didn't want to hurt her anymore. The only thing I asked of her was not to keep my daughter from me, and she promised she wouldn't. But she has.

Because of my prior sentence for the crime I didn't commit, I was under "Three Strikes," and that resulted in two consecutive 25-to-life sentences. My lawyer tried to talk me out of the plea bargain, and the judge wouldn't accept it two days in a row, and only did when I agreed to say the reason for it was to avoid an even more severe sentence. So I said that, but my reason was not to hurt Sharon anymore.

That decision hurt more than all of my past combined. Besides losing my freedom for more than 50 years—for a total "crime spree" of $150—I've lost my wife and daughter, the only good things I ever had.

* * * * *

I cope now day-to-day, struggling with my loss. Thoughts of one day seeing my daughter is what keeps me going. I hope she hasn't forgot me.

I still feel that pain of my parents' abandonment. What I "heard" from that—what I still "hear"—is *"You're not deserving of a humane childhood. You're not worth the love and affection children deserve. You're nothing, and it's all your fault!"*

Accompanying my pain is a tidal wave of anger and a strong desire to compensate for the love and affection I was denied in childhood. The little boy inside is still trying to find his mother to take care of him. My entire life has been devoted to secretly satisfying my childhood needs, from drugs to an unhealthy marriage, which—in a twisted sense of reality—my wife became a surrogate parent.

I will never understand the act of child abandonment, or get over the pain that comes from it. I would often say to myself, *"I would never abandon my child?"* Yet, I wonder how she feels about me.

* * * * *

I see myself as a decent man who believes in God. I'm not the monster the courts made me out to be. I know my true desires as a human being. I don't want the pain of my past, just the joy to love and be loved. It almost sounds too simple, too dramatic, but it's the truth of my life.

Until the drugs came along, I made my wife a good husband: loving, caring, compassionate, neat, clean.

I'm a fragile, emotional, loving person—fragile is the key word. I'm very needy. I don't like to use that phrase, but it's honest. God knows that about Curtis, and he's put some good support around me right now.

I lack trust about life and people. Oh, yeah, yeah! That's the main thing. What my parents did to me created the idea that I'm unworthy to be loved, that I'm not lovable, that I'm a bad person. Knowing in my head that isn't true doesn't make any difference in how I feel inside.

I'm very possessive. I want to hold onto everything I get because I've never had anything I haven't lost. I'm always afraid anything that seems good will go away. It's hard to trust people who seem to care, but, if anyone knew Curtis, they'd understand and be able to accept that.

I've never entered therapy. I've always been afraid to find out what a screwed-up person I am. I want to believe I'm a good person, but I'm afraid I'm not.

* * * * *

What gives me a lot of joy and a feeling of worth right now is base-ball. I can't get enough of it! Look at the scrapes on my face, and legs, and arms! Just like in high school, I'm "Mr. Baseball" here. I've got the trophies from our prison tournaments in my cell.

Why baseball? I'm not sure. The only time my family was together and there was no arguing was at Little League. Maybe my baseball is the search for myself. Maybe, somehow, I think, *"If I play well enough, maybe they will come."* I don't know.

* * * * *

Prison has also given God a chance to get at me. I've been running, and running, and running, but prison has stopped me, and given God a chance.

What gives me meaning right now is seeing how God is healing me. He's started way back—like with my parents—and is moving toward the present. There's a woman who works in the chapel who has the same first name as my mother. I've always avoided her for that reason. A few weeks ago, though, I asked God for the courage to talk to her. I really felt the need, drawn, but I was afraid. God gave me the courage, and when I did, I just started sobbing. She just held me. Somehow, it was like my mother holding me. I can feel a change.

God has put some good friends into my life lately. They know Curtis, and validate that he isn't a monster. I don't think there is anyone outside these walls. There is a couple who have been writing to me through the chapel for two years. They've told me I'm like a son to them, but they have never come to visit. They only just recently gave me their home address.

My love for my daughter was a culmination of my past, a joy for the moment I had with her, and a goal for the future. She means everything to me, and often is my motivation to go on. I've never seen her since I entered prison. My wife promised not to keep her from me, but now it's like I don't exist. Sharon has gotten a divorce. I've written to her and my daughter, but there is never a response. I pray for my daughter and ex-wife. I believe, if I'd discovered God's healing power earlier in my life, I'd have them now.

God is an important part of my life now. I'm learning to take all I've been through and give it to him. It's not easy, but he's my only hope. I thank God for the little I have left. I don't say I don't have doubts at times. It's a growing process, and I have a lot to learn.

*   *   *   *   *

I question how much God will allow me to take. I question the scripture where Jesus promises I won't be given more than I can handle.

I want the truth to come out. I don't deserve a life sentence. God, being love, won't allow it. I want to give God a fair shot. I want to trust. But look at my life!

I don't have any goals. I take one day at a time. I'm waiting for that point when I can't handle this anymore, when Curtis is so beaten down he can't take it anymore. Part of me wants to hang-on for my daughter, but I've had days when suicide seemed the only way out of the pain.

God is teaching me to cope with my past without the unhealthy elements. It's tough. Without God, I would probably be dead right now. I can't stand the thought of living the rest of my life with what I've been through. God has given me the strength to go on, and the hope to keep going. I've come a long way, but I still have a long way to go.

God and my friends are helping me to heal, but they are not taking the place of my family. There's something about family nothing else can take the place of. In 1981, my mother told me, *"You're looking for a fictitious family."* I don't believe that. I'm looking for someone to love me like Sharon did.

* * * * * * * * * * * *
* * * * * * * * * * * *

Curtis is a living, hurting indictment of California's "Three Strikes" law. As sad and tragic as his personal story is, the inequity of his life sentence cries out for justice. This is a young man who has never destroyed any property, never used a weapon, never injured anyone—or even threatened to—who will be in his seventies before he even becomes *eligible* for parole. He never was, and is not now, a danger to anyone. He had a drug problem, not a hardcore commitment to crime.

It took me half a dozen rewrites before I could put Curtis' legal story together in a way that made sense, because it doesn't make sense! It was difficult for me to believe his situation, because the punishment is so out of proportion to the crime. I decided to advocate for him, *to* him.

I offered to write a summary of his criminal and legal history for him, and to obtain the names of several law professors he could contact for possible assistance or leads. He knew the odds of anyone responding were slim, but he was energized by my willingness to help him. He felt it would be worth the effort and cost just to help educate future jurists as to what the law can do when it loses rationality.[20]

＊ ＊ ＊ ＊ ＊

A good part of the reason Curtis is in this untenable situation has to do with what my lawyer told me when I interviewed him after my arrest, and asked about his fees: *"You get the justice you pay for."* Curtis couldn't pay anything, so he was represented by a well-intentioned, but inexperienced and inept, stretched-thin public defender.

---

20. From Curtis' letters to law professors: "I have no family nor resources to work on my behalf. I am hoping you might have a student who would be interested in taking on my case as a class project. If not, I hope you will be able to use it in your teaching. Future lawyers, judges and legislators need to understand from real life how unjust 'justice' can often be."

Added to this major defect (which is built into the criminal justice system as a whole) was the great sorrow Curtis felt for the effects of his legal problems on his wife and daughter. In his "love story" eagerness to end the proceedings, he sacrificed himself to spare them. It took three hearings on three consecutive days before the judge would allow him to plea bargain the process to an end. That is because his primary concern—to spare his wife and daughter any more grief—was not legally acceptable. He was required to give a system-reason, rather than a heart one:

Court: So it would appear to the Court that the negotiated settlement was based on the fact that if you had gone to trial, the longer sentence would have been a possible 90 years-to-life. Is that correct, sir?

Defendant: Well, that's not why I did it, but that is correct. I'm getting a shorter sentence, but that's not the reason I'm doing this.

Court: All right. And what is the reason why you're doing this?

Defendant: I didn't want my wife involved in this at all. I've hurt her enough. Not that she was involved in any of the crimes. It's just that they had subpoenaed her to come to court. She doesn't need that.

Court: You've indicated that one consideration for the plea is the fact that you felt that you've hurt your wife enough and that you don't want her to have to be a witness—a possible witness in the case. Would the main consideration for accepting this negotiated settlement be that you received a sentence benefit? In other words, you're going to receive—if you go through with this—you're going to

	receive a sentence of 50 years rather than the most likely 90 years to state prison. Is that the…
Defendant:	Well, I'm not going to get out on either sentence, you know. That can't be the main reason, but that is—it's part of it, yes. But, you know, you know what the main reason is. I understand what I'm doing.[21]

This willingness to sacrifice himself is another insight into Curtis' nature, and, as with everything else about him, it is complex. Mixed together are his sense of himself as "unworthy of love," his deep need to be loved and to love, and his childlike tendency to lead with his heart. This psychological amalgam frequently manifests itself in his outer passivity at injustices done to him.

* * * * *

Because of the many years he has left to serve, Curtis was transferred to a more secure prison in July 1998, after a failed escape attempt by two other inmates. (The system fears that, since they have nothing to lose, those without hope of release will attempt to escape.) Curtis left in tears, as he was leaving his only "home" and its limited, but supportive, sense of belonging. There were tears in the eyes of some of the staff, as well, inasmuch as many realize the travesty of his incarceration.

* * * * *

Curtis floundered in his new restrictive environment, cut off from his few close friends he had left, confined to his cell for much of the day,

---

21. Taken from Curtis' sentencing transcript.

with limited access to chapel, no prospect of getting a job because of his security classification, and no baseball.

After not having seen his daughter for four years nor having received a letter for 1 1/2 years, he learned that his former wife had moved and left no forwarding address. He sank into a prolonged depression.

> *"It's an awful feeling waking each day to darkness. My health has suffered because I won't get out of bed to eat. My prayers are filled with questions. It's not that I'm asking God to free me, or give me lots of money. All I ask for is a letter from my daughter. I've fallen back to times of uncontrollable tears. Sleep gives me temporary peace."*

A cousin of Curtis established contact for a while, and came to visit. She led Curtis to believe his mother would be receptive to hearing from him. So, with very confused emotions, he reached out one more time, only to encounter silence. The cousin promised to send money and a care package. They never came, and neither does the cousin anymore.

In early 1999, I was taken aback by Curtis' elated announcement of his engagement to a woman in Florida whom he knew only by mail and phone. I was hard-pressed to respond to his excited, *"Are you happy for me?"* I fudged my concern by answering, *"I'm happy for whatever happiness comes your way, but I also have a lot of questions to ask?"* I raised issues for his prayerful reflections, and asked very pointedly, *"I very much understand what it would mean to you to have someone to whom to belong, but what would motivate Kristy to commit to a marriage in which you may never live as a couple?"*

A few weeks later came his heartbroken news that Kristy had disappeared without a word of explanation or farewell. After some effort,

Curtis learned that Kristy had quit her job and was getting ready to marry a former boyfriend. While my heart hurt for Curtis, I was grateful that it had ended before he could invest more of himself.

I was encouraged and impressed by how Curtis processed this latest rejection and abandonment. Rather than fall into a bottomless emotional pit, he shared his pain with those he trusted did care, and over a period of six weeks, he was able to move on in a healthy and hopeful way. *"God has used you to be the vessel that brings me much love—not only yours, but Mrs. Joan's, Sr. Carol's and Fr. Steve's. As I sit here with or in a few of my heavy down days, I cannot deny that **I am loved**."*

* * * * * * * * * * * *
* * * * * * * * * * * *

We've all experienced being part of a card or board game, or participated in a sport, in which one of the players announces new rules, or reinterprets old ones, *after* the play has been completed. Even in such a fun context, the unfairness easily leads to tension.

California's 1994 "Three Strikes" legislation developed out of increasing public frustration at the rising crime rates of a decade ago, and a frantic attempt to contain it.[22] The concern was legitimate, and remains so, but the response has been out of proportion to the problem,

---

22. Under "Three Strikes," previously committed serious or violent felonies are "strikes." With one strike, conviction for *any* new felony requires double the normal sentence; with two strikes, a new conviction requires a *minimum* of 25 years-to-life. District Attorneys are allowed some discretion in not charging prior felonies as strikes, but judges have little leeway.

and has become progressively unjust in its application. The rules keep changing after the plays have been made.

Inasmuch as most politicians decide what they believe about an issue by reading the polls, "tough on crime" has become the frenzied battle cry of the poll-watching legislators. The TV hit-ads accuse opponents in the most absurd and unfair—but effective—ways of being "soft on crime." That invective has become the "kiss of death" to political careers.

Related to this, has been the "Me first!" panic which hits the legislature after every isolated, but particularly heinous crime, as its members fall all over each other attempting to be the first to sponsor the bill which will create a new crime, or increase the penalty for the old ones. This knee-jerk approach to legislation has eliminated rational reflection, and the input of less impassioned and more informed considerations.

Fanning the flames has been the aggressive tabloid-bent media, which by comparison, make even the legislators look statesmanlike, as they climb and claw their way toward capturing the most gruesome footage, and shove their invasive microphones into the faces of grieving victims. One glance at the TV listings for any day of the week is enough to show that crime and "law and order" sell and build ratings.

Even though crime rates have fallen dramatically in the past few years, crime continues to be the major drum-beating issue of both politicians and "news" choreographers.

Criminologists have yet to determine the causal relationship between "Three Strikes" and the drop in the crime rate. However, I have no hesitancy in attributing a major role to it. (It is a major topic of conversation and concern among my companions here.) It has removed many habitual and dangerous criminals from the streets, and kept them off for long periods. I even support that goal of "Three Strikes." But, as with the controversial drift nets which indiscriminately sweep the oceans scooping up anything that swims, along with the sought after marketable fish, "Three Strikes" lacks the discernment mechanisms for separating habitual, violent criminals from those who have committed isolated crimes—there is a big difference in both the type of criminal, and in the type of person involved.

While Curtis is a particularly egregious example of "Three Strikes" gone awry—50 years-to-life for non-violent crimes of stealing a total of less than $150, and possession of a small amount of cocaine for personal use—his is not a rare situation.

The glaring injustices in the current application of "Three Strikes" include:

1. **the lack of distinction in sentencing** between career criminals, who need to be incarcerated, and people, who, if given drug rehabilitation, mental health care or skill training, could soon return to society as contributing, taxpaying citizens;

2. **retroactive application** allows a crime committed 20 years prior to the enactment of the law to be counted as a "strike;"

3. **multiple punishments for the same crime** takes place when a "strike," for which a person has already served 10 years in prison, mandates a second 25 years-to-life sentence;

judges are severely limited in seeking to adjust draconian, mandatory sentences in the interests of proportionality and justice.[23]

A legislator, compassionate enough to risk the "soft on crime" label, seeking to mitigate the blatant injustices of "Three Strikes" sentences, can count on the "jungle justice" response of some colleagues, such as the *"I don't care if they only steal a Tootsie Pop!"* retort an enlightened East Bay legislator recently received for just such an effort. Such a closed attitude gives new meaning to the concept of "blind justice."

If humane and justice considerations are not enough reason to rethink and redesign "Three Strikes" law, perhaps financial ones will eventually force a restructuring. Besides the current annual expenditures of $4,609,000,000 to run California's prison system for 162,000 inmates, consider the additional billions that will be needed as new prisons are built to handle the ever-increasing numbers of new inmates annually incarcerated in facilities averaging nearly 200% of capacity now.

Consider also, the cost of maintaining an increasingly elderly population of prisoners requiring medical, geriatric, "nursing home"-type care. Remember, a 25-to-life sentence means a person is not even eligible to be *considered* for parole for at least 18 years, and, under the current, highly politicized Board of Prison Terms, it is the "to life" part of the sentences that is the norm.

* * * * *

23. Bob Egelko,"Judges Get Less Leeway," The Sacramento Bee, 6 Jan. 1998.

There are others, besides Curtis, who languish in prison for the lack of money (read "inability to pay for justice"), or a functional family to offer love and support, or a compassionate advocate. "Hope" should not have to depend upon "luck" or "blessing," but, too often, it does.

Benny—"I Just Went With the Flow"

Benny is 30, but his short, prematurely graying hair and moustache give him the appearance of 40. He is 5'9", muscular, athletic and heavily tattooed. His face is a study in contrasts—it mirrors his inner and outer struggles to find his place in the world, and in the hearts of others, as well as within his own.

Benny's dark, penetrating eyes betray his pain and sadness, and his fear of losing his life's lately-acquired love—and the subsequent hope it has enkindled within him—in the face of what could minimally be another 18 years of incarceration. His eyes simultaneously probe and plead. I found myself wanting to say something in response to his silent searching of my thoughts and feelings, but I didn't know what was being sought.

His eyes can also quickly revert to the defensive coldness and control, out of which, for most of his life, he has protected himself from his gentle side. His taciturn gaze is discomforting—it is both a test and a dare.

By contrast, Benny's ready smile conveys his softer side. He is never alone in the yard. He is a natural leader who attracts others by his presence, which radiates strength and quiet acceptance. Perhaps it is his unchallenged power that allows him to reach out in a protective way to the weak of either body or mind. He does so with a jovial, unaffected kindness, without ever compromising his unquestioned machismo. He is always in relationship, but he never gets close.

Benny's smile and eyes never seem to be totally in harmony. Each opens a window into his soul, but both together do not contain the whole. Benny is caught between the hope toward which his heart is calling him, and the temptation to revert back to the "security" of not feeling and not dreaming anymore.

* * * * *

I met Benny's mother when she came to visit on Easter. It was her first visit in a long time. While waiting in the yard to hear our names called announcing visitors, Benny and I chatted. He was anxious, both out of excited anticipation (*"She said she'd be here rain or shine, no matter what."*), and out of disquietude that she might not come—he had been set up for disappointment many times before. He tried to be nonchalant, as though it wouldn't matter one way or the other, but from having listened to the hurt and anger in his voice when he talked about those disappointments, I knew otherwise.

Benny's mother is about his height, very young looking and attractive. The waiting for the visiting page was a death/resurrection moment for Benny, as it ushered in a full afternoon of intense sharing between them in a far corner of the visiting area. Afterwards, he told me, *"I needed that. We talked about a lot of important things. She still can't accept that I have such a long sentence, though."*

* * * * *

"It doesn't matter," a shrug and a half-smile, and a glance of searching, hurting eyes, are Benny's ways of summarizing how much things that touch him most deeply actually do matter. That amalgam masks his hurts and disappointments, and his unsuccessful attempts to shield himself from the anxiety that surrounds his hopes and expectations. *"It doesn't matter,"* was scattered throughout his sharing about his family

and Maria, whether anyone was coming to visit, or whether anyone had written.

✳ ✳ ✳ ✳ ✳

Benny had previously sent the first draft of his story to his mother, as a way of sharing himself with her through a medium that allowed him to open up—from a distance. He reported, *"She tripped out! She told me she had new hope for me, because she didn't think I could open up to anyone. She said, 'You've always had a good heart, but you could never let it out.'"*

✳ ✳ ✳ ✳ ✳

It took a few listening sessions before I could make sense of my notes about Maria. Although Benny wears a wedding band, and referred to her as his "wife," there was no mention of a marriage. Maria is the mother of Benny's four year old son, and his yo-yo relationship with her has tested him on every level of his being, giving him moments of great hope and joy, and times of tremendous heartache and despair.

Maria has touched Benny's heart as no other person has, and liberated so much of his buried self that he has come to realize both how much tenderness and neediness is in him, and how capable he is of ruthless rage—his power and his powerlessness.

Over the past two years, Maria has moved from tenuous commitment to distant silence, and back again, like a ballerina leaping and pirouetting in all directions, while her suitor waits on bended knee for her return. There are mutual attraction and distrust, as well as the fear of investing too much lest it all be lost. Maria has experienced Benny's darker side, and knows from a previous marriage what it is like living as a married "widow" of a convict.

When Benny speaks of his son, he glows. Little Benny is the one true love of his heart. He writes to him every week, and saves his small prison salary to send home for clothes and toys. Benny clings to the rickety bridge connecting him to his family.

* * * * * * * * * * * * *
* * * * * * * * * * * * *

I grew up in Pomona. My family offered me a lot. My parents were together, and we shared a lot of good things and times. I was happy when I was young. I didn't see the hurting part of my family then. As I grew older, people seemed to separate. When my parents separated, I blamed it on myself. I was really hurt by it.

My mother is a really good person. We have always been close. She has always been there to spoil me, and to help me get things I needed. She tried to do her best—she gave me so much love and affection! I was too stubborn to accept it. I don't know if I didn't see it then, or if other things were just more important.

She bragged about me to her friends. She told them I was going to be a nerd—that's because she was proud of me because I did so well in school. I tried to make her proud, too—at least through junior high. No matter how many times I rejected her, she has always been there for me—she still is. She still does what she can.

I know she's hurting now—her only close son got sentenced to life. I can read between the lines in her letters. She's feeling, *"Somewhere along the way, I did something wrong."*

* * * * *

My dad is a spray painter. He was there when I was growing up, but not like other dads I've seen who do the basics. When I was between 5–7, he got me involved in T-ball and karate, but that was about it. My dad sometimes took us on rides to the mountains, or to a ranch to do shooting. We went to a lot of family gatherings, but, mainly, it was my godfather who took me camping and did things with me. We never had a father-son talking. He was always closed up.

When I was in elementary school, I couldn't understand how he could give another man (principal) permission to scold or paddle me, instead of doing it himself at home. As I grew older, we grew apart.

*   *   *   *   *

I have an older brother, but he was always gone, and I don't really know him.

I had a sister five years younger. She died when she was 19, the last time I was down. It took two weeks before they notified me. It was a big loss, and it caused me to lose my mental state. We had been really close. We talked a lot, and I could give her advice. She looked up to me. I really felt bad.

My baby sister is 14. We don't really know each other either, since all of her life, I've been in prison. She was with me, though, all through the trial. She came to court, and gave me a lot of support. She couldn't believe it when I got life.

She's sentimental and is afraid to come to see me, because she is afraid she'll cry. I tell her, *"That's okay, we'll cry together."* I used to think that, too, that men don't cry. I could never do it anywhere else—it would have been seen as weakness.

I don't want her to see life like I have. I try to help her to grow up right, to be constructive, and to push education. I try to use my life to point her to better things. I've told her my lifestyle says it all. It would hurt me most to lose her. Besides my son, she's all I have.

* * * * *

I got good grades until high school. I liked math and English, but not science or history. History didn't pertain to anything. I didn't care what happened 150 years ago; I wasn't there. I didn't play sports, but I was always good with my hands. After I do something a couple of times, my hands seem to adjust to it. I took wood shop and graphic arts; they were neat.

I didn't have any goals for the future. I've never really had any real plan for my life. Whatever group I was with, I'd go along with whatever they wanted to do—for better or worse. I just went with the flow.

* * * * *

I had a negative attitude when I entered high school. No one could tell me anything. In high school, I had an image change. I had friends in all the groups, not like in elementary school, when I was just with the educated kids. I cared about the things people would say about me because I hung around the educated kids. I always seemed to hang with those with negative attitudes, and who'd always find reasons for cutting school. I wanted people to notice me, and to feel, *"Don't mess with him!"*

In the middle of the 9th grade, I got expelled, because I was always getting into fights. I had the option of alternative school until noon, or home study. I tried alternative school for a while, but then I started fighting there, too. Then, I went into individual study, and met with a teacher once a week. I quit going to school in the 10th grade. I got arrested for the first time that year, too.

* * * * *

I was around drugs all my life. When I was small, my uncles had pot. I saw it, helped to cultivate it, and put it into bags. I started pinching a little to have some of my own. I began smoking pot when I was 13.

In junior high, I was selling pills, and, by the time I was 15–16, I was selling heroin and cocaine. I began using cocaine then, too. It became part of a lifestyle that let me buy whatever I wanted, and to have girls— you know. I had power in my pocket—more money than most people could dream of. I sold in order to use it, and to have enough to spend on what I wanted. I broke even. I never saved anything, or planned for the future. I only thought for the day—just partying, having no responsibilities, and no one telling me what to do.

I got carried away abusing it—like, I'd take off for a couple of days and not come home. Or, if I came home to sleep, even for a few hours, I'd have this feeling, *"I'm missing something. I've got to get back out there!"*

My family began to notice and approach me, trying to help me, asking me to stop. I said I didn't want to. Being as young as I was, and being high, I couldn't think straight. I seemed to have everything I needed. I felt, *"I can handle it. I'm not addicted."* I wasn't like the worst addicts I knew, I didn't steal from my family.

* * * * *

When my dad asked me if I was selling, I denied it. But, since he knew, I figured it was time to leave. I was 15 or 16. I wanted to lessen my disrespect for my parents, and I wanted to live the way I wanted to. They were asking too many questions, and I didn't want to bring problems on them, like the house getting shot at in retaliation from other gangs.

I lived with an aunt for a while. As long as she didn't see it, and I didn't sell it from her house, she wasn't bothered. I did all my business at the park down the street.

*   *   *   *   *

I started pulling away from my family because I was always wondering what I was missing. I was looking for excitement. I started hanging with friends in the neighborhood. I lived in a gang environment. I didn't have to go looking for it, it was all around me. I just grew up doing gang stuff. My uncles were involved, and my grandma's house got shot up once. I knew once I started with the gang, I had to leave my family, so they wouldn't get hurt because of me.

My gang was not very big compared to most—maybe 20-30 guys. It was better that way. You could feel the closeness—knew who was who. In the gang, you could feel power—do what you wanted to do, and get away with it. You didn't have to worry about who would get you, because they were there for you, and you for them.

We went looking for trouble, did things for retaliation—just to get away with it, just for the fun of it. Nine out of ten times, I would do things by myself. There was always a lot of excitement, getting high, lots of girls.

I don't know if I've actually killed anybody. I've been in situations where I've shot someone from five feet away, but I never stayed around to find out, or thought about it again. I just did what had to be done.

* * * * *

My first arrest was for armed robbery. A friend, who worked in a restaurant, planned the job. He set it up, and decided who would do what, then he stayed home. My partner and I intercepted the restaurant manager when he came out with the money at 11 p.m. I approached him in the parking lot and said, *"Give me the money!"*

My partner, the car driver and I got away for a few hours. We split the money four ways. Then my partner remembered he had left the gun in the car. Someone had seen the license number, and, when we got back to the car, there were 7–8 cops waiting.

I was 16 then, and ended up with three years probation. I had a part-time job at McDonald's for a few months before that. When I went back to work, they wanted me to take a polygraph to see if I had been stealing from them. That hurt me.

Actually, the job was a cover for the money I was making selling drugs—which I continued to do—so my parents would connect the things I was doing and buying with my job. They were happy that I had it, and started letting me make more decisions. I could tell them I'd be late at work, then go do what I needed to do. I didn't get bothered by the deception, because, when you start using drugs, you learn to block out a lot of things from your mind; you begin thinking, *"What will benefit me?"* You don't care what anyone else thinks or has to offer.

* * * * *

I started giving distance to the homeboys, and started selling drugs big time. I wanted to make money, and the more I made, the more I wanted. I had a greed that was unstoppable. I didn't take money from others, but I made enough on my own.

I wasn't too involved in the neighborhood anymore, but then a situation happened when I was 17 that led to my first term. I had been partying, and I was drunk. A friend was driving me home, and in the middle of an intersection, another car pulled up on my friend's side, and the guys started yelling gang slogans. I didn't pay any attention for a while, because I wasn't in the mood. But, they kept following us and keeping it up. I finally got fed up.

I pulled my gun from my waist, reached over my friend, and shot the driver of the other car. They were lucky, because the gun jammed, otherwise I would have shot both of them.

It all happened in broad daylight, and someone got the license number again. I got six years in the Youth Authority for two counts of attempted murder. I was very scared for the first few months, because I didn't understand the system, and I had heard stories of people getting raped and stomped on. It was hard to face the reality of being there.

I got to know people, and started getting involved in criminal activities and selling drugs. I got the drugs from girls who would come to visit me, and from other guys in there. Money talked. I started living comfortably and forgot the outside world.

I began to pick up a hardened heart from so much negativity flowing through there. I started rejecting the people who loved and cared for me. If someone would say, *"We'll be there to visit,"* then not show up, I'd stop calling. It was partly to punish them, and partly to protect myself from getting set up then hurt, because I'd get a worried mind that something bad must have happened to them. I'd do the same thing when things weren't going my way, or I didn't get what I wanted.

*   *   *   *   *

I never let anyone get close before; I never trusted anyone. This is the first time I've learned to open up. I couldn't before, because it would have been taken for weakness. I'd feel, *"Who am I to open up to another man about what I'm feeling?"*

I had one special girlfriend when I was 16–17. It was my first long-term relationship. I saw how my father was to my mother, and my grandfather to my grandmother, and that's the way I was with her. It was hard for me to express how I felt. I'd buy her things, but I couldn't say, *"I love you,"* like girls like to hear. I took her to the movies and things like that, but it wasn't enough. I didn't come through for her when she needed me.

I tried to hide that I was doing drugs as long as I could, but she eventually found out. One day, she came over unexpectedly. I was in the garage weighing and bagging, and she walked in. She got really upset and hurt, and started yelling, *"So, this is where everything has been coming from!"*

A lot of trust was broken. The relationship gradually eroded, and finally ended when I got locked up. She came to visit at first, but she was brokenhearted, and couldn't accept not having me with her. I spoiled her.

*   *   *   *   *

When I got out in May 1994, I started seeing someone I had gone out with in junior high. I was already running a wild life that wasn't going anywhere, and I knew I'd end up either dead or in prison. I don't know why I went to Maria's house when I got out—maybe it was God bringing us back together. She was on her lunch break, and we went out. She was shy and timid. She was involved with someone else, and had been married to a guy for six years, who was in prison then. They had four kids together.

I started seeing her on occasion. Her mother took a liking to how I was with the kids. She and her husband were going out of state, and asked if I would stay with Maria to help with the kids. I said, *"Sure!"* After they came back, they invited me to come with their family to their cabin in the San Bernardino Mountains. That's when it all started, and I moved in with Maria in November 1994.

When I left Y.A., I made the decision to turn my life around. And, when I started with Maria, I was doing real good. I was working 10-12 hours a day at a good job. The bosses liked me and the way I worked. I had a good position and was responsible for opening up at 4 a.m. and turning off alarms. A couple of times, I was late because Maria didn't want to get up to take me to work, and I didn't want to leave her with the kids without the car. My bosses warned me about it, then finally let me go. That was in February 1995, and, after that, things started going downhill again. All I really knew how to do was street things, and I started selling drugs again.

Things started going wrong between us, too. I'm the kind of person who wants things done. I'm very impatient and stubborn. She supposedly had married this guy in Las Vegas. In January, we went to check the Los Angeles County records, and then went to Las Vegas. They told us she could file for an annulment, because he was jailed a few months after the marriage.

I was getting frustrated because this hadn't been done, and I started dragging her down. She has filed, but the paperwork still hasn't all been done. If that had gone okay, I'd probably still have my job. It still pisses me.

* * * * *

Maria is a very good person with a big heart. She always went out of her way for me, and spoiled me, too. I'd see something in a store that I liked, and, the next Christmas or birthday, she'd bought it for me. She was always trying to make me happy.

I seen I could manipulate her in a lot of ways. I was doing my own thing, and told her it was none of her business. She didn't want me doing what I was doing, but I stopped minding her. I told her if she didn't want to put up with it, leave. God only knows why she put up with it—I would have left. I was never home, always leaving. It was so easy to verbally abuse her.

I put up a wall, because I felt her getting close. I knew she knew what I was doing—trying to push her to the edge to see if she'd leave. It scares me when I feel someone getting close. The only ones who have stayed with me are the ones who love me—the ones I hurt. She didn't break or leave. She stood by me giving me the love I didn't want out of fear of getting hurt.

My wife tries to come to visit, but she works hard trying to take care of the family by herself, and it isn't easy for her to get here. She didn't come for my birthday, and I got upset with her on the phone. That made her upset. She says I don't understand how it is for her. She doesn't understand what it's like for me! I don't know what to write to her, because I'm afraid I'll hurt her feelings. She didn't expect me to get a life sentence. I put myself in this situation.

I got involved with someone with kids—it trips me out! Who knows, I might never have found someone like her. Until I met Maria, I didn't know what love was. When I was a kid, "love" was just a word. She has to love me to have put up with my attitude, verbal abuse and mistrust. We've made it this far, I'm sure we'll make it.

*   *   *   *   *

I had a callus on my heart, and my life was filled with negativity and mistrust. I was always loaded, not paying attention to anyone. I was so frustrated with life. I would stay up all the time until I burned out and hallucinated. I let my anger out on other people.

I didn't give any thought to the hurt I was causing. I just did what I wanted to do. I neglected my old lady, the kids, my family. They couldn't understand why I backed away. All I knew was how to survive on the streets. I wanted to just get by. The faster the day went by, the better— another day gone. On drugs, the last thing you think about is caring for other people. That's the worst part of it all. I didn't see what reality was—my mind was so polluted by drugs and negativity. I knew I'd either become hooked, or go back to prison.

There were times when I fought toward reality. Times when I'd get sober and wonder what it would be like, if I got it together. But fear would take over again. I didn't know anything but the streets, and I didn't think I could make it. I was afraid I'd fail and disappoint my family. I went to other people for assistance, so, if I failed, I could blame them.

I wanted to be something at one time—wanted to be my own person. I'd think, *"What can I do? What can I be?"* It hurts now to realize how much of my life I've wasted. I look around here and see people who don't seem like they belong here—people who have done things in their lives who were in business, have kids and grandkids. I wonder, *"Why are they here?"* I was young and stupid.

* * * * *

I went back to prison in November 1995 for possession of methamphetamines. I got 25 years-to-life on "three strikes and you're out." Twenty-five-to-life for nothing! It just doesn't seem right. It's unjust, but it woke me up. Sometimes I think maybe I deserve what I got for all the bad things I've done, but, then, I get confused with how that fits into repentance and conversion. It's on appeal, but otherwise the earliest I could get out is 2015.

* * * * *

I'm separated from my son. I never thought I'd be. He is seventeen months now. He was born since I've been down—I've never been with him. I took on a responsibility for him, and for my wife's four kids. I knew it was going to be hard to be separated from them, but, when my son was born, it became a whole new thing.

The way I was raised by my mother and father, and grandpa, was that, if you have kids, be there for them and with them. My son isn't experiencing family. It's real hard for me to call home. I talk to my son, but he is only able to say "yes" or "no." I avoid phoning because it hurts so much.

In her letters, Maria tells me she misses me so much. She sees my son, who is identical to me, and he reminds her of me. My dad brought baby pictures of my son and of me—you couldn't tell the difference!

Maria works as a cashier in a grocery. Her oldest girl and a boy are in school. Two other girls are in childcare, and my son is in another childcare. It isn't easy for her. She's great with the kids, though. They are her life.

* * * * *

When his son turned two, Benny's mother brought Benny's son, as well as Benny's sister, to visit for the first time. It was the "softer" Benny who showed me Polaroid photos of all of them together and who shared his aching joy: *"I was afraid he would be scared and cry, but, when he saw me, he ran to me with his arms out, yelling, 'Daddy!' I held him and hugged him, and the tears were coming. It was so hard to let go again, and to watch them leave."*

* * * * *

The last time I was doing time, I started going to church and Bible meetings. Then I'd miss a day, then another day. I wasn't ready to hear it. One time, a guy came on Friday nights and explained what he was going to do, and invited us to participate. I enjoyed that. In my heart I wanted to follow Christ, but I wasn't paying too much attention.

When I got out, I was excited about being out, and overwhelmed with that. I put my Bible away. No one around me was going to church, so I had no one to go with, nothing to follow.

* * * * *

From being born and raised Catholic, what I learned in Y.A. was a totally different way of knowing Christ. As a child, I went to First Communion classes. I had perfect attendance and got a Bible. It was like school. I was a child. It was a ritual, and I did what my family did. I didn't understand what God wanted to offer me.

Because I was an altar boy, I was involved. The teaching wasn't "today" teaching—you know, what's happening in this present time. It's like Catholics live out of that book the priest reads from. "Church" for me now means "congregation." Now, I know Christ in my heart, and that is what's important. Now it's personal—I know about prayer, and I know that it works.

Doing time, I've seen all religions. Basically, it's what you feel in your heart, and how you come to know God. For me, Christ has been in my heart, and helped me deal with my pains and confusions. I believe God is blessing me here, and my family and my kids.

I've been reading and studying the Bible for two years now. I believe, and I try to follow it, and to accomplish its goals. That's a very hard decision to make because of the lifestyle I've led. People can mock you and put you down: *"Maybe he is weak and hiding behind religion?"* That makes me angry.

If it wasn't for my faith, I'd be a very hateful person right now, because of the situations I've been in. Now, I'm able to get along with other races, and cultures different from mine. My heart is kind, and I'm able to be patient with my problems. Christ has helped me overcome a lot.

* * * * *

My communication with my father is better now. I never thought my dad would write me letters and say the things he has. On the phone, it used to be "yes" and "no," and no conversation.

I never saw him really cry, except when his father died, and the two times I was sentenced to prison. This seems to be the time for him to open up. I try to offer him understanding, love and Bible verses to encourage him.

He tells me he prays, and I think he goes to church. Now, his letters show love and affection—all the things I missed growing up. It's good! It's never too late. I believe it is Jesus doing it. Believing in Jesus is the biggest thing I've gained from religion.

* * * * *

This time around, I've decided to avoid as much prison lifestyle as I possibly can. God understands I'm in a negative environment. One of the biggest things to overcome is to leave street life, to cut off homies and friends, in order to seek a better life. I decided not to get involved in gangs and the underworld—I don't want anything to do with that anymore.

Those connections have enabled me to stay alive, not to get hurt, and to stay out of fights. By leaving that behind, I've made a choice to present myself as a better person this time around—not to seek power, or to try to earn respect.

* * * * *

I'm not trying to accomplish education goals. My main goals are my legal fight to get out, to get closer to God, and to be reunited to my family and kids. While I'm here, I'm trying to be as close to them as I can, and to share with them what love is all about.

When I get out, I want to be better. I want to be a loving, understanding father, showing my kids love and affection. I want to help them get on the right track, to get a good education, even if I have to struggle for every penny.

I know the things that lead to the street lifestyle. My tattoos are evidence of the life I've lived. They show the pain and death I've seen, the drugs. They're the art of what my life has been.

I want to rebuild what they've lost. They feel betrayed, that no one loves them, because both their dad and I left them. I know they feel they did something wrong.

I'm not going to be into wanting cars, house and fancy things. I know *now* that all I need is the love of family.

It's hard when you leave, though, too. After prison, you are dead to society. You can't get out and present yourself as a human being—you're a criminal. It makes no difference what your crime was. You don't get any credit for the changes you've made, or for what's in your heart.

*   *   *   *   *

I see people in here who have it good. They have loving families, get visits and packages. My family and I are very close. Some of them write, some of them don't—but I expect them to. At the same time, I try to cut them off, so I can concentrate on being here—on my work and church. It distracts me when I think about them; it makes me worry about them and what's going on out there.

My family support is good, but they don't understand my need to program my life to handle the time. I'm the one doing the time! My expectations of them are too high, but why can't they all put a little bit together, so they can send me something every month. I know they have their own lives and bills, but, shit, they throw money away! It's hard to make it in here.

＊　＊　＊　＊　＊

In some ways, I feel myself going backward again. The worst part of doing time is being hard and mean to people—having to put up a front. I don't want to go backward. This is the place to work on how I'm going to live when I get out. If I ever mess up again, there is no use thinking I'll ever get out next time.

＊　＊　＊　＊　＊　＊　＊　＊　＊　＊　＊　＊
＊　＊　＊　＊　＊　＊　＊　＊　＊　＊　＊　＊

Benny speaks of a "hardened heart." It is a common and complex prison malady. Woven into it are the learned survival skills that gradually dissolve trust and empathy for fellow inmates, as well as build protective walls against the disappointments caused by family and friends on the outside. "Out of sight, out of mind," is a truism many inmates feel and experience.

Many of the men have "burned" the hands and hearts of those who have tried to care for them, and many know that, yet the hoping that someone still cares never dies. Mail is distributed during afternoon lockdown. Every man is at his door watching as the tier officer moves from cell to cell. "Rainbows" surround those places where he stops, while "dark clouds" hover where he passes. When the days without mail become weeks, and the weeks become normal, the heart calcifies to anesthetize itself from the hurt.

The vast majority of men never hear their names included in the visiting pages. To make it even harder, those names heard week after week, soon become a familiar litany, tearing off the numbness-scab and exposing the loneliness of those never called.

*　*　*　*　*

The search for spiritual solace is another conundrum for Benny. St. Augustine could have had Benny in mind when he penned, *"Our hearts were made for you, O Lord, and they are restless until they rest in you."*

Before most of the prison is awake, Benny is up reading his Bible, praying and pondering. He doesn't want a hardened heart, and he struggles for that "heart of flesh" which he knows God alone can create in him. In 1999, he went to classes to prepare for Confirmation, hoping that would help. I watch him at Mass, as he listens intently to the scriptures and preaching. He prays and sings with concentration, as though seeking the "missing link" in the words. I can almost feel the energy he is expending wanting "something" to fall into place, to "fix" all the confused relationships with his family, to allow him to leave prison and be with them, and to put his spirit at peace.

It is not easy to "put on Christ" in any context, but everything in prison is the antithesis of Gospel-based living. Benny has the inner strength to stand against the crowd, but he also knows that, if he is going to spend the best part of his life here, he cannot stand totally apart either. His head and heart pull him one way; his background and depressing situation tug him in another.

*　*　*　*　*

Early in 1999, an elderly nun "adopted" Benny. Sr. Mary James has become his postal-godmother, providing a safe and caring ear for his confused heart. She shared Benny's story with a nephew, who then wrote offering to send Christmas gifts in Benny's name to his son and sister. When the letter arrived, an incredulous Benny sought me out on the yard. *"What is this? Who is this guy? Why is he doing this for me, when my own family won't?"* None of this fit into Benny's life-experience categories. I responded, *"Benny, you've been praying and praying. Can't you see God reaching out and loving you through these people?"* He smiled and shook his head, *"This is too weird!"*

A week later, Maria made a surprise visit—her first in two years—and brought Little Benny. By coincidence—or Providence—Benny was in the visiting area when they walked in. He had volunteered to be Santa's helper at the annual family Christmas day, never expecting his own son to be there. Once again, he was incredulous. He was able to get a truck for his son, who paraded it proudly around the room, *"My Daddy gave me this truck! My Daddy loves me!"*

The visit allowed Benny and Maria to air some of their hurts, fears and hopes, and Benny ended the day in an excited, joyful, anxious daze. For the next month, Benny and Maria were in frequent phone and letter communication. Then Maria's mother (with whom she lives) had a phone block placed on the collect calls. When Benny writes to his son every week, he encloses a note to Maria, but responses have become rare. Once a month, Benny's mother takes Little Benny to her home so Benny can call and talk with him.

The last time we talked, I hadn't seen Benny for a few weeks. He told me he had been pulling back from spending time in the yard and with his homies. He told me, *"I spend a lot of time staring out the window. I think of my son. He doesn't have a father. If I had killed someone, I'd be able to tell myself, 'Okay, you deserve to be here the rest of your life.' But not for what I did."*

Will he spend the rest of his life staring out the window? Will he never get to be the father his heart aches to be? These two questions constantly haunt Benny and keep him precariously teetering on the precipice of despair.

* * * * * * * * * * * * *
* * * * * * * * * * * * *

The relationship of drugs to criminal activity is particularly clear and convincing in Benny's life. He speaks of having lived in another world, in which others shared only peripherally, and in which nothing else mattered.

Another aspect that Benny shares is that of how drug use affected him psychologically and relationally. Under the influence of drugs, nothing and no one else had a claim to his loyalty. Loved ones of addicts need to know that if they get in the way between the addict and the drug, they will lose. Any romantic thought that "love will conquer" is naive, not because the addict lacks love for them, but because the addiction is all consuming of an addict's energies and focus. The drug addict does not choose and act rationally, let alone from affection, because he is captive to his addiction—satisfying its insatiable demands is his only concern and goal.

All of the men who are sharing their stories with you, have spoken of the major role drugs have played in bringing them to prison. In this one aspect of their lives, they are "typical" of 80% of inmates.[24] Whether

---

24. "Alcohol, Drugs Linked to 80% of Inmates in U.S.," The Sacramento Bee, 9 Jan. 1998. A report of the National Center on Addiction and Substance Abuse (Columbia Univ.).

their involvement with drugs began as a way of coping with, and dulling psychological pain, as a source of easy money, or because of peer influence, the result was the same: once the addiction was established, and the criminal activity began, they were prison-bound.

None of these men support the popular conviction that "light" drugs, such as marijuana or "recreational" use of drugs, does not lead to heavier drugs and addiction.

All of these men know and state, without reservation, that getting started on drugs was a major—if not *the* major—reason for them being incarcerated. All of them have sworn to put drugs behind them when they leave—many made that same pledge the *last* time they left prison, too. Many discover how easily good intentions surrender to addictive patterns of coping, when confronted by too much pressure, temptation or discouragement. Drugs are merciless jailers that do not recognize "time off for good behavior."

The men who are genuinely committed to breaking the power drugs have over them struggle against the temptation to succumb even in here. Drugs are available in prison, as Armando shared, and "pruno"[25] is a popular substitute for bottled alcohol. Many attend Alcoholics Anonymous or Narcotics Anonymous meetings, but professional drug rehabilitation is offered to only a small percentage of those needing it.

California's first serious commitment to prison drug rehabilitation began in Richard J. Donovan Correctional Facility in San Diego County. The program lasts 6–8 months, and continues with a support

---

25. Inmate-produced alcoholic drink fermented from breakfast and lunch fruit.

program after inmates are paroled. A study showed a 16% recidivism rate for those who completed the aftercare program (as compared to over 70% system wide who were not in a rehab program).

As a result of the success of the Donovan program, which treats 300 inmates, another program to treat 1,400 has been established at Corcoran State Prison. In 1998, the legislature authorized another 3,000 beds for new programs in other prisons.[26]

"...*the nation's current emphasis on punishment, rather than treatment, is fundamentally flawed and a costly mistake.*"[27] While the criminal acts that lead to prison need to be appropriately addressed, imposing harsher and longer penalties on people who need medical and psychological treatment makes little sense from humane, financial or public safety considerations. The "logic" of this approach is similar to that of the policy of the former Soviet Union, of committing political dissidents to mental hospitals. "*Policy makers weigh public opinion more than they weigh science.*"[28]

---

26. Andy Furillo, "Prison Drug Treatment Unpopular, But It Works," The Sacramento Bee 4 Feb. 1999:A1.

27. "Drug Addition Is Treatable," The Sacramento Bee, 19 Mar. 1998:B10.

28. Ibid, Dr. Phillip Lee, UCSF Medical School.

Darcy—"Is That Hope?"

Darcy could pass for a young John Denver. He is tall, slightly built with a fair complection. His dark blond hair is parted in the middle, and is combed to the sides to meet his collar. His moustache modifies what would otherwise be a totally youthful 34, and his round, wire-framed glasses create an image of a student-choirboy. Even his voice tones and cadence convey a childlike quality.

Darcy began a journal in 1995, while waiting in the county jail for trial and sentencing. In it, Darcy captures his spiritual and emotional insights, turmoil, pains and joys at given moments. Selections are woven into his story as glimpses into Darcy's ongoing process of discerning his relationship to the people, and the meaning of the events, which are his life story, from the perspective of later therapy and reflection.[29]

Darcy's three stepbrothers, especially the younger two, were his founts of acceptance and affection. They were all older, and all shared the erratic, abusive treatment of his mother during the long absences of their father. Partly from the natural adulation of a younger boy toward older ones, and partly from emotional deprivation, Darcy sought their companionship. They accepted him and included him in their activities.

The youngest brother molested Darcy over a prolonged period. That relationship continues to confuse him. Even now, as he is able to

---

29. Selections from Darcy's journal are enclosed in [brackets].

rationally distinguish abuse from affection, he is unable to sort out the conflicting emotions of love, hurt and anger.

As he communicates these—and other—very personal and embarrassing events from his life to a virtual stranger, I am aware of how much trust he is placing in me, and how vulnerable he is allowing himself to be. I find myself simultaneously listening to Darcy and to my own internal feelings. I am feeling for him and with him, and admiring his courage.

Darcy tells his story with disarming openness and trust. His sharing is soft-spoken, laden with feeling, and is like listening to a child speaking from its heart. His facial expressions and eyes bear testimony to his words. He has obviously come a long way, through a tortured and confused life, and it is clear that the process is still underway. His warm, sad eyes, and slight, genuine smile seem to be asking, *"Can you listen to this and still accept me?"*

* * * * * * * * * * * *
* * * * * * * * * * * *

I had a memory of myself in the womb. Even then, I felt I wasn't wanted. I asked my mother how she felt when she found out she was pregnant. She told me she was angry with God because she was pregnant, that she didn't want a child, that she didn't want me.

I've tried all my life to be wanted and loved. I can adapt, and tell you what you want to hear in order for you to accept me. I learned that with my mother. It was like I lived two lives: one thing on the outside to please, and a secret life within with my real feelings.

* * * * *

My first memories are of my grandmother. I don't have any memories of my mother until I was four or five. Grandma would hold me and sing to me. She was good to me. I lived with my grandparents a lot—my mother's parents. I loved going over there because they spoiled me.

When I was very little, we lived in a small lumber town in Humboldt County. My dad was a logger. But, my folks divorced when I was two, and we moved to Fresno, where my grandparents were.

[When I woke up this morning something struck my mind. I believe I know why my attachment to Bud, and that idea of love, was so strong. I remember when I was around three or four, I lived at my granddad's and grandma's in Sanger. I remember how Grandma used to hold me, hug me, rock me, and sing to me. 'Twinkle, Twinkle, Little Star,' 'Jesus Loves Me' and other songs. I remember feeling so loved and so safe. I loved those times. Oh, Grandma, thank you for the love you gave me! I believe that after my mom took me, and we moved to Oregon, I had a void, a need for love. I know I didn't get it from my mom. Most of my memories are of a cold scary person. I believe when Bud (stepbrother) did those things with me (molested him), I grabbed on to fill a void in my life. I believed that that was the love I so badly needed.

I just called my grandma and told her how much it meant to me when she used to hold me and sing to me. I thanked her.   (5/31/95)]

* * * * *

My first memories of my mother are from when I was four, and she remarried. We moved to Oregon. I remember being in this big van with her, my stepfather, and three stepbrothers, who were 10, 11, and 12.

I know from listening to family talk that a lot happened to me during this the time I was four or five. I don't remember a lot of it, but, since I began therapy, I've been able to remember feelings from that time.

Many of my memories of my mother are of her being angry. I know that I loved her, but I was afraid of her. She got angry a lot, and I was always trying to do right by her.

Many of my early memories of my mother are of her arguing with my stepfather. Once when I was four or five, she called me into her room. She was really angry, and I was afraid. She told me to lie down on the bed on my back, and to stay there. She started loading a 22-pistol. I asked her if she was going to shoot me. She snapped back, *"No, I'm not going to shoot you! That would be stupid!"* She went out of the room, and I could hear more arguing, and then shots. I just stayed there really scared. She never talked about it afterwards, and I never asked. My stepbrothers talked about it, though, but I can't remember what they said—just that it didn't feel good.

I remember lots of outbursts of anger from my mother, and things like her slapping me, pushing my stepbrother over at the table when he leaned back in his chair, and her having boots on and walking down the hall kicking holes in the wall.

She didn't allow crying. I wasn't allowed to show feelings. Whenever I did, she'd say, *"Why are you feeling that way? That's silly!"* I learned to bury what I feel, and to change what I was feeling to something acceptable.

At the same time, Mom did a lot of things with me. She brought me a horse once, and one of my brothers would put me on behind him and take me for a ride. We played games as a family. But, she wasn't consistent. It was really confusing with her going on and off. There was always a lot of pressure. If I did things "right," she'd like me; if not, she didn't. I'd try to do the things that made her happy, so she'd like me. I was always fearful, scared of how she got when she was angry, even when not at me. I was always afraid of doing something wrong.

[Dear Mom,

I've just finished crying and still hurt. I was so hurt and angry toward you for I felt put down and rejected! I'm not going to stop writing and giving out the 'gobbledygook!' I have poured out my heart to you, grandma, and those I love, and, if this—or I am—not good enough, then you can just be unsatisfied and judgmental if you want! It took some time for what you said to hit me, and it really wasn't that big, but it did touch a nerve of the many times I've been hurt, put down and how I felt, and what I was, or where I was, was not good enough for you. All I've shared and written has been from my heart, and if you choose not to believe in me, or that I have shared the truth, so be it. You are not responsible for how I feel right now yet I was hurt, and believe my emotions and experiences, my life and who I am, was again rejected as you have rejected me so many times before. Even before I was ever born, you did not want me! Well, my Lord wants me, and he has given me great spiritual experiences and signs of his love. Many friends and brothers in Christ do want to hear my 'gobbledygook,' and are deeply touched and moved by it!

I have chosen to forgive you, but I do not want to pull punches or hide truth. In other words, I am willing to bare hurts and risk being hurt in a relationship with you, for you are my mother and worth having a relationship with, even if it is not the deep personal one I desire where I can bring all my personal 'gobbledygook' to you without fear of being rejected, or not good enough, or where you think I should be.

Where I can be right or wrong with you, and not be criticized. Where you look to see me, and not what you perceive about me. I don't need you, and almost wanted to just tell you I didn't want to see you, but that wasn't true and was wrong. I just hurt that much. As I write this, I don't even know if I should send this to you, for this 'gobbledygook' is my feelings. It is part of me, even if all of it doesn't make sense yet. I knew I had to write it, and my feelings are not wrong, and it is not wrong for me to share them with you.

The choice I must make is if it is best for all of us to share them. I need to express my feelings, and, if not to you, I know my Lord understands and will receive me just where I am. I can't change how I feel and who I am for you or anyone, even God. All I can do is be willing to change and open to growth, and walk with my Lord as he changes me.

If you do not desire to share, or are unable to at this depth and level, I desire you to let me know in a kind, considerate way. I will find—and do have—others I can go to with this, and will share myself with those who are able to accept me. Yet, I still desire to have this depth with you.

May our Lord, in his grace, mercy and everlasting love, bring you into the depths of his love, so you may see me with the eyes of our Lord, and I may do the same for you.

I love you, Mom!—Your son, Darcy   (4/27/96)]

*   *   *   *   *

I liked having brothers to play with. I could approach them with things easier than my mom. I wanted to fit in with them and be accepted. I liked it when they included me in things. The older boys had motorcycles, and they'd take me on rides. The middle one used to spend time with me, helping me put models together. He was very patient with me. Sometimes, if I'd scratch his back, he'd let me pick one of his toys to play with.

When they would do things they weren't supposed to, I'd tell on them. I told on them a lot. So, when they would drink beer, they'd make me drink some, too, so I couldn't tell on them, because I had done it, too. I wanted to be with them, so I did it. That's how they broke me from telling on them.

* * * * *

Bud, the youngest, spent a lot of time with me. I liked that. I wanted his love, like I had with my grandma. He began to molest me. He would do things to me, and then have me do them to him. I really don't remember the first times, but my mother told me about one time she looked into the bathroom, and he was naked and I was on my knees.

My first real memory of being molested was when he told me to keep what we were doing a secret, because our folks would get mad. Knowing my mother, I did. It went on for about five years, until he ran away when he was 15 or 16.

I was confused about it, but I know I liked it; it felt good. I know I really loved him. A lot of the other attention he gave me, and times he'd play with me were neat. I wanted to be with him, and he included me in things. I think he really did love me and cared for me, but there was a lot of junk mixed in with the good. I still haven't sorted it all out. I'm still confused about it. I know I really loved him—I still love him, but there is anger there, too.

When Bud came back, after running away, he was my hero. I was always closest to him. We've never talked about what happened. I've never confronted him.

* * * * *

My stepfather was very passive. I like him. He was a truck driver and was gone a lot. Sometimes he'd take me on trips in his truck. We did take family vacations camping and backpacking. I have some good memories of our trip to Yosemite when I was seven.

My stepfather never abused me. Sometimes he'd say things that would hurt, but that was mostly when he was fighting with my mom.

* * * * *

I liked school and did really well. My brothers helped me with my ABC's and learning how to count; so did my mom. It was fun.

My favorite teacher was in the first grade. She spent a lot of time with me, and encouraged me to write. She told me she really liked my stories, and had me read them in front of the class. I remember one was "Me and an Ant Named Fred."

I got along really well with the other kids. Me and another guy were leaders. I had a lot of friends until I switched schools in the fourth grade, when my mom and stepfather split for awhile. I was small, and in the new school, the other kids picked on me a lot. One time a group surrounded me and provoked a fight, while one boy got on his hands and knees behind me, and another kid pushed me over.

I was there for fourth and fifth grades. Another boy and I became friends, but I never really fit in there. I went back to my first school for sixth grade, because my folks got back together again.

* * * * *

When we went to church as a family, we went to my stepfather's. He was a Seventh-day Adventist. When I was with my grandparents, I went to my grandfather's Southern Baptist Church—the same when my folks were split. It was really confusing. My folks had lots of disagreements over religion. We always went with my stepdad's ways, though.

By the end of my elementary years, all my brothers had run away, because their dad was gone so much, and my mom was so controlling. She was verbally rough on them.

When I felt bad, I'd go out and play by myself. I had my own little world of soldiers and heroes. I played the role of the hero in whatever games I played.

* * * * *

My first memory of my real father was when I was about four. An aunt and I went to pick him up at a bus depot. He was just getting back from Vietnam, I think.

When I was growing up, I visited him in the summers, but I never felt close to him—for no reason on his part. He was busy with work, and would be gone a week or two at a time, logging. He just didn't have much time.

He tried to make contact over the years, but I didn't respond. I felt I needed to get better first. We didn't get to know each other, because I didn't want to go to him until I was good enough, successful. He worked hard, had a good home, etc.—I didn't feel on a par with him. I want him to be proud of me, and I'm not proud of me.

When I was 16, I went to live with him for nine months in Redding. I was running from problems with my mom, and was already into drugs. I was looking for something. He was gone a lot, but I worked around his place. I like my stepmother. It was a positive time.

He lives in Oregon now. When my wife and I went there for his father's funeral, my dad talked a lot with my wife—real close—but not with me. I felt jealous. Later she told me it was all about me. He wanted to know how I was doing, and was concerned about me, so he talked to her. He'd do the same thing through letters to my grandmother.

I called him from jail the last time. I felt really ashamed, but he was very supportive, and he told me, "Everyone fouls up sometime." He sends me money now.

We are just now starting to relate. Even on the phone today, it was awkward for both of us. But, we're working on it.

* * * * *

I got started on drugs when I was 14. One weekend, my mom and stepfather left me alone for the weekend. I had wanted to go with them, and I was feeling hurt and left out. I just rebelled in anger.

I invited friends over. We decided to go get drunk. I got bombed. We took my mom's car—I didn't have a license, and I was drunk—and we drove around.

That was the start of a pattern. I started giving up a lot of things, and began getting drunk on weekends.

Before that, friends had offered me pot, but I had refused. The summer before I went to live with my dad, while I was visiting him, my stepsisters were smoking pot. One night I wasn't feeling too well and didn't think I could handle alcohol, so I started smoking with them and their friends at a party.

When I was real young, my mom had found some pot my brothers were growing in our yard. She dragged me out to it and told me, "You see this stuff? Don't you ever touch it, or I'll break your arm!" I know she was trying to teach me to stay away from it, but, at this point in my life, whatever she was against, I was for.

I had my own car when I was 16. I was making $700-$1,000 every winter helping my mom sell Christmas trees, and I worked off and on for my grandparents. The money supported both my car and my pot habit. I was smoking regularly, and started going to high school high. My grades began to drop. When I went the next summer to live with my father, my stepsisters were still partying and getting high, and I joined them. It's the freest I've ever felt!

Pot was the start of my serious drug addiction. Mostly, I used it with Bud.

*   *   *   *   *

When I was a senior, I began hanging out with a stoner, and listening to a lot of rock music. I gave up my goals for college and aeronautical engineering, and started doing cocaine on the weekends, as well as pot all of the time.

After high school, I got a good job making bags for cement. As a reward, my grandparents gave me a car. I was still getting high all the time, mostly with Bud, who was into coke now, too. I really got hooked. I was doing it so much, it wasn't having its effect anymore. My nose was plugged up from sniffing it, and I had to use a straw to inhale it at the back of my throat. But I wasn't shooting it yet, so I kept telling myself, "I won't become a junkie as long as I don't shoot up."

One day, I was with a friend who was shooting, and he told me to try it. I did, and I started going downhill fast. That's all I'd do. I lost my job, sold my car and everything else I had to buy coke. My savings were gone, my computer, my radio-controlled planes—everything.

In an attempt to help me, Bud went to my mother and told her how bad I was. That really pissed me off. My mom came to see me, and I was ready to fight. I was expecting her to be angry and yelling, and I was determined that nothing she said was going to get to me. Then she leveled me with, "I love you Darcy. What you are doing is wrong, but there is nothing I can do about it. I'm here if you need me."

That threw me off track emotionally. I didn't know how to handle it—I'm not sure I believed it.

I started getting even deeper into drugs. I began stealing things from my mother. I took things I knew meant something to her, her microwave and Kirby vacuum—she always was telling people how she loved her Kirby.

I got $60 for the microwave, and I was driving with a friend to buy dope with it, when I started feeling guilty about having stolen from my mom. I knew I couldn't spend the money. I told my friend, "*I can't buy dope with this money.*" He started getting angry, putting me down, and calling me names. This was one guy I thought accepted me and was my friend, and he was putting me down because I couldn't steal from my mother. I started crying.

We got to where we were going, and he went in and bought his drugs. All the way back to his house, he kept putting me down. He screeched to a stop in the driveway, slammed the door, and went into the house. I was still sitting in the car crying.

I got out of the car and fell on my knees on the lawn, and cried out to Jesus to help me. I can't explain what I felt, but I felt the burden leave me, and I felt relieved. I went inside and told my friend what happened, but he wouldn't believe me. He had calmed down some by now, and offered me some of his coke, but I refused it.

I left and went to my mom's, and told her what I'd done. I gave her the $60 and the Kirby. After that, I started going back to church—my mom went with me. It was the start of my way out, but I had a long way to go yet.

* * * * *

I met my wife, Carol, through a mutual friend when we were at her mother's house getting high. It was like a crack house—you know, people always there doing drugs, and it was always a mess and not kept up—it was like our house was later. I was 21 and Carol was 15, but I thought she was older. I asked her mother, "*Who is your roommate?*" I thought she was cute, and we ended up talking all night. I felt really comfortable with her.

My friend and Carol's mom set us up. My friend told me Carol had a crush on me. We started dating, and did for quite awhile. I was living with my mom, but we weren't getting along, and I ended up getting kicked out, so I moved in with them. My worst drug abuse years were with them.

About a year later, I asked Carol's mom if I could marry Carol. She said, "*Yes, but what am I going to get out of it?*" She was on welfare, and getting extra money for Carol. Not long after that, Carol and I walked out into an almond orchard one day, and talked about what it meant to get married, and what it meant to each of us. We made up our own vows, and exchanged them out there. Two years later, just before Thanksgiving in 1989, we got married legally.

* * * * *

Both of us were caught up in co-dependency, and we reinforced each other's addictions. Besides the alcohol and drug addictions, there was sexual addiction, too.

I started my sex addiction with Bud. Then, when I was a teenager, I started going to adult stores to get pornography. I had a few minor affairs. I had clung to Bud because I needed to believe in something. I didn't think I could be man enough for my wife because of my experience with Bud, and my need to be accepted by him. I ended up clinging to Carol the same way—to belong to someone, to be okay, to feel okay about myself.

Carol had been sexually molested by her father, so she was messed up sexually, too. It was one more way in which we reinforced each other in a negative way.

[I realized why my wife couldn't respond when I shared all my sickness and molestation issues with her that first time. As the counselor put it, she was carrying so much pain she could not hear my issues without feeling all her pain from her life. She just didn't have the resources to be there with me and for me. I realize how I had held that against her and never really consciously realized it.
  (6/20/95)]

Drug use led to my sexual addiction being activated, because I'd only act out when I was high. I had inner conflicts about my sexual urges, and I could not have acted them out without the release of the inhibitions. The drugs provided that release. Carol would start or stop using drugs whenever I did.

* * * * *

After awhile, I got tired of drugs, and, for the first time, I got sober on my own. Through my mother's boyfriend—she had divorced my stepfather when I was 18, five years earlier—I got a good job in Long Beach as a gas tester. I made $10 an hour.

Carol moved down to join me, and we had a nice apartment. I wanted to leave the past behind, and I had a goal of a family and a different kind of life. I thought I could make the change on my own, but I wasn't dealing with the issues I needed to face.

My insecurities began showing up at work, even though I was doing well and getting good reviews. I started doing drugs again to overcome my feelings of inadequacy. My bosses began to see the signs of the drugs' effects, and in November 1990, I was finally fired.

* * * * *

Nine months before losing my job, Carol had been pregnant. One night after we had been up for three days, high on crank (speed), we got into a car accident. I was driving and was so totally spaced out, I had driven twenty miles past where we lived. We were on our way back, when the accident happened. Three weeks later, Carol had a miscarriage. I blamed myself for that.

With the job gone, we moved back to Fresno. It was the toughest point in my life to that time. My dreams were gone. We had nothing. I started going to AA, and we were able to live in a small area in the back of the AA club in exchange for Carol running the club. I got a job at McDonald's, which was a real blow to my self-image after the good job I had blown.

I was going to AA, but I never shared anything about my sexual addiction. I didn't fully comprehend the depths of my problems, though my problems were caused by the drugs and alcohol. I'd be sober for three months, then relapse; then sober nine months, then relapse again. That went on for almost three years.

* * * * *

After six months of running the club, we were told we'd have to move on. The job was meant as a temporary assistance to help people get started, and they didn't want us to become dependent upon it.

We moved in with a guy who smoked pot. About the same time, my oldest stepbrother disappeared because he was being sought on rape charges. (He's still on the run.) The stress of these things led to the next relapse. I started showing up to work smelling like pot, and ended up getting fired. I didn't care anymore at that point. I had given up. Carol was working at a fast-food place, but we had to go on public assistance for the first time.

During this time, we found out Carol was pregnant again. We got ourselves straightened up, and moved in with her mother. But, people were always there getting high, so we moved into another apartment after I found another fast food job. It was the first place of our own since we left Long Beach.

Our son was born in May 1992. As happy as I was, my next relapse came from the pressure of trying to be a father. My mother was criticizing everything I was trying to do. According to her, I wasn't doing anything right.

Pot was always my first resort to cover up my feelings when pressures built. It was a pattern I'd learned as a teen. And, as before, pot led to more.

[I was watching Rescue 911, and saw stories of children, a premature baby. So precious is the life my Lord gives! I remembered Carol, my son Aaron's birth, which was so special to me for I was sober. Being with my wife, seeing her true strength come through, and being able to have some part to encourage her to go on. I cried so deeply. Also the other stories. I thought for my family, yet, later, believe it was for deep hurts of feelings I still remember. Also, many times my mom was so angry and mean, not letting me feel my feelings, or be myself without threats of violence which struck such deep terror in my heart. (5/3/96)]

It wasn't long before my mother called the police on us, and Carol and I were both arrested for being under the influence of methamphetamines. The charges were dropped, but we lost custody of our son for a few weeks, until we got into a parenting class—which was really good, because it talked about a lot of things that helped me as a person, not just as a father.

I relapsed again six months later, and abused my wife bad over porno. We'd been high for a week, and I was enticing her sexually, and wanted her to entice me—like Bud and I had done—but she wouldn't. I needed her to help me feel okay about what I was doing. I had always done what my mother wanted me to do, and I expected her to do the same for me. I was hitting her with the metal vacuum cleaner tube saying, *"You're going to do what you promised! You're going to do what I want!"* I really hurt her, and knew I needed help. No charges were filed.

* * * * *

I had been involved in a church, and soon after my bad relapse, my pastor and another man from the church stopped by to visit. I told them what had happened. My pastor asked me, *"What are you going to do about it?"*

When I was a teen, my mother and I had gone to a counselor named Roy, who was connected with the same church. I had heard him at church give testimony about how God had cured him of his heroin addiction. I admired him and thought he'd understand, so I went to him and told him everything, including about a couple of times, about eight years earlier, when my wife and I had molested her little brother, who was about 11 then. Both of us knew it wasn't okay, but we gave each other "permission"—another aspect of our co-dependency.

The "adult" in me knew that Roy would have to report me, but the "child" in me needed to tell everything. He reported me to the police, and, a few weeks later, I was arrested and charged with one count of child molestation. My wife was charged with one misdemeanor count of sexual abuse. That was in November 1992.

Carol and I were on welfare then. I had been working for a man from the church, doing things around his place. The arrest was hard to take at that point, because I had been really trying to turn things around. I was going to a Christian-based AA group, and both of us were going to a church group which dealt with sexual addiction issues. I got angry at God and at my counselor, too, because he was upset with me, and was accusing me of not being fully open with him. I wasn't. I was still in denial about a lot of my sexual addictions and experiences.

I continued counseling with Roy for about a year, while going through the court process. I stayed sober about fourteen months. I ended up getting probation and work furlough. Besides my groups, I went back to college, too. I bit off too much and was beginning to feel the pressure building again. I was trying too hard to please everyone, and to do everything right.

At the same time, Carol was beginning to react to what I was sharing about my past. It brought all kinds of memories and feelings in her about her own experiences, which she hadn't dealt with. Both of us relapsed for about six months, starting around Christmas 1993. Again, I got angry with God for not "fixing" me. During those six months, we were both off and on about therapy. I realized I was at a critical point. I'd seek help, but, then, I'd run when facing things got too scary. I had tried so hard to please everyone, and now it seemed futile. I was burned out, and just wanted to give up.

[I just realized why I cry every time I see things in movies or TV that deal with love or family! I feel the pain of being molested and a deep desire to be really loved, to have a loving relationship the way it should be.

More pain and more hurt! I've been cutting off and changing my emotions. I've been trying to gain happiness through things that today only bring me destruction. They used to work. I used to be happy but the pain keeps getting bigger and bigger. I robbed myself of how I really felt to protect myself from something I could not bare. Oh, what pain! Oh, what loss! Please God may I not have lost it all! (5/14/95)]

The leaders of the therapy group made us agree to strict conditions before they would let us back into the group. One was that Carol and I had to agree to a separation, because we were too caught up in each other—too enmeshed in each other's problems and needs to help each other. So, we agreed on a date when we were going to separate.

We were still on welfare, so I reached out to different church members looking for a place to live. I explained my situation, but no one got back to me. The deadline for separating was getting close. I was getting frustrated and angry, and was feeling pressured, so I relapsed again, and verbally abused her.

[I remember the time I got in trouble, and my mom yelled at me and sent me to bed. I remember lying in my bed feeling so sorry for what I had done. I don't even remember what it was. I just cried, sobbed deeply, I was just hoping wishing my mom would come into my room hug me and tell me everything was OK, that she loved me. I wanted her love to know I was OK. I wanted to be forgiven. I cried, felt rejected, withdrew, felt responsible, felt unloved and worthless. I see many of the same things today, except I cry less, and get angry in its place.   (5/15/95)]

Then, in June 1994, I remembered the commitment I had made not to abuse her, and I stopped, but I told Carol she couldn't leave me. The pattern always was, that, once I got sober, the violence was gone, and I buried all the hurt and anger again. She put a sign in the window, though, saying she was being held captive, and the neighbors called the police. I was arrested, but the charges were dropped and I was released three days later, because they didn't know I was on probation.

It took me a week to be able to reach my probation officer. During that week I looked for the toughest therapy program around, because I had stopped going to the groups after my last relapse. My probation officer told me to turn myself in, though, and, after two months in jail, he put me into a Salvation Army program.

In September, I met a new counselor in that program, who worked in the county jail helping men deal with sexual issues. He was older, and I really related to him and trusted him. I started doing one-to-one therapy with him and began dealing with the real issues for the first time in my life. Pat was like a father figure for me. He asked questions without being invasive. I started to really open up. Each session I'd be in tears, and feel all kinds of hurt, but, afterwards, I felt better. I still held back about Bud. I had an overwhelming fear of the buried emotions about my abuse, and I was afraid of facing the truth. I also loved Bud, and didn't want to feel anger at him, which I was afraid I would, if I really faced our relationship. I was still running.

* * * * *

Carol and I had taken trips, during which we'd escape from everything for a few days of drugs, pornography and sex. I convinced her to take "just one more trip" for my birthday in March 1995. We went to San Francisco. When we came back, though, we didn't stop.

I started getting abusive again, and ended up hitting her with the vacuum tube. This time is was a plastic one, though. While I was hitting her, I was saying to myself, *"This is because you don't love me!"* She did, though. What I was doing was pouring all my junk out on her. I was arrested and charged with three counts of spousal abuse and one of assault with a deadly weapon.

I spent two months in the county jail, while the legal process was taking place. I was still seeing the counselor from the Salvation Army.

[I have to write about an incident that happened about a week ago—I got a taste and glimpse of the pain, terror, confusion my wife went through. I had a cellie who was evil, possessed or influenced by demons, the things I let into my family. I started to get to know him. Sometimes you could talk with him and he would make sense. Yet, late at night he would get strange, waking up laughing, saying things that made no sense. At first, I didn't know if he was trying to intimidate me or what. One night I woke up from a dream about my old life. It hurt and I hated it. He was listening to headphones. I could hear the rock music. I think it woke me up. He was asleep, so I reached over to turn it down, bumping the headphone jack. It woke him up. He said, *'What are you doing?'* I responded, *'Turn that down, it woke me up!'* I didn't say it nice, yet also not angrily, kind of grumpy. He went off! *'Who do you think you are running things?'* He threatened to stick me even, and I responded, *'Hey, don't threaten me!'* I finally didn't respond. I was angry and scared not knowing what I should do or how I should handle things. He threw my things off the shelf to the floor, then tried to blame me and make me pick it up. I did and said similar things to Carol. I just got a glimpse of what I put her through.

Well, he picked up the stuff and threw it on my bed. He apologized later. I forgave him. The next day we both had to apologize to our neighbor for waking him up at 3:00 a.m. A few days later it happened again. Yet this time he woke up laughing and saying strange things like 'legion.' At one point he asked, *'Are you awake?'* I said yes and he blamed me for waking him up. I tried to speak easy and calm him, but he only got worse. I decided to be quiet and not answer. He made no sense. He got angry and was standing over me calling me all kinds of names, like 'fag,' mocking my Christianity. I decided I would do nothing unless he came at me. He was standing on his bed over me when a guard came. He calmed. While he couldn't see, I made motions to the guard with my finger to my head that he was crazy. The guard asked if I felt safe. I shook my head no. He called the sergeant, yet my cellie calmed down, so they figured everything was OK. Not long later, he started again. Oh, I forgot, the first time he slapped me, I did nothing. I prayed.

Well, as he started going again he said he was going to kick my ass. He knocked my glasses off and reached out to grab me. He started to swing at me, and I raised my arms to block. He pulled out of the punch then started to accuse me saying, *'What are you trying to do? Why did you jump up so quick?'* He was acting like I was provoking or trying to start something with him. That's when he knocked my glasses off, and when he reached for me, I grabbed his wrists. He pulled back saying, *'What are you doing?'* When he pulled away, I stood on his bed and tried to grab him and hold him. He tried to gouge my eyes out. We bounced around, and I fell in a bad way, my head and part of my shoulder hanging off his bed. I was under the chain of his folding bed and he easily pinned me. I was, and felt, helpless. I had no leverage to get him off of me, no room to turn or roll. He kept deriding me, then hit me in the side of the head several times. I cried out to the Lord for help. The guards came, and he quit.

They took him away. They had to take me also, and I spent the rest of the night and half the next day in the hole, with only a half size blanket and my boxers, not even my glasses. It hurt so much. I realized—and believe the Lord showed me as I prayed—a glimpse of what my wife suffered by what I went through. It was so confusing and there were moments when fear gripped me in terror, and, when I was pinned, I felt so helpless, vulnerable and weak. I don't think I'll ever completely realize what my wife suffered at the hand of the one she loved the most. O God, I cry as I write this, and realize the pain, terror and suffering of my wife at my hand!   (9/29/95)]

* * * * *

During one of my sessions with the counselor while I was in jail, I had that memory of myself in the womb. I was feeling unwanted and unloved. I saw a hand come down and place a crown on my head. It wasn't a big one or a fancy one—it was very small. I experienced that as acceptance by God—that *he* wanted me and had a plan for me, even before I was born.

After that, the knot which always seemed to be in my stomach, disappeared, and I didn't try as before for my mom's approval. I still wanted it—I still do—but I don't need it like before. I don't have to perform, or try to earn it anymore. For the first time, I felt that the pain outside me was greater than the pain inside me. I felt encouragement and able to face the pain—to give it all to God. Facing prison a few months earlier, I would have just given up.

[I hurt again! I just got off the phone with my mom. When I was working through the book the other day, I realized my mom's part in letting this happen. I wrote her a letter holding her to making excuses. I think I jumped the gun. I think deep inside I expected something to happen, a restoration. It's too soon. I have more to work through. I hate what she's done. She hasn't really loved me like she should. She keeps putting others first because she can't face and admit she's wrong. I hurt and hate her for that. She's so cold. She can't understand, and I can't share my life with her in a proper way like it should be. That hurts. (5/22/95)]

* * * * *

I was sentenced to two concurrent terms: six years for child molestation, because I had violated my probation from that charge, and six years to the two spousal abuse counts, plus a two year enhancement. So I'm serving 80% on eight years on two strikes.

* * * * *

Entering prison looked bleak. At Wasco, we were locked down 23 hours a day. My cellie was always talking about rape and molestation. The guy next door was a Christian. He gave me some spiritual support. I did a lot of praying, read the Bible, and continued keeping the journal I had started in county jail.

In August 1995, I came here. I started going to chapel. I prayed for friends, and I started finding some in the yard. After awhile, I got involved with Yokefellows, which is a group of inmates who meet to share what is going on with them, and to support each other in prayer and friendship. That got me more involved in chapel.

I joined a second Yokefellows group for sex offenders. It was rough at first having to become real with what I'd done. All of the abuse titles were hard to accept, because I don't see myself that way, but that is what I did. I have a lot of shame in me about the things I've done.

I found myself starting to let old patterns develop of doing what was needed to be accepted. I had to work through that. The group really helped me grow in the ability to be concerned about others, instead of just myself.

Prison has been a miracle for me—so different from what I had expected it to be. The Lord has given me so much here. I started working in the shoe factory. Now I'm in electronics. I hope to move into data processing. It feels good because I've quit so many things in my life.

I started playing baseball at 32! I never thought I could play in school, and I wanted to quit this time, too, but I'm improving and getting *genuine* feedback, rather than manipulating for it. I want to learn to play, so I can teach my sons.

[Dad, I ask for your help, your mercy and grace to be poured out on me! Lord, I broke my little finger today and got hit in the face with the ball. Father, I'm not afraid, and I'm overcoming my fears, and I really want to play ball and improve. I left myself out as a kid, or was left out and gave up. I fought, and still fight, mental battles. Lord, I want to grow, to overcome! O Dad, please grant me skill! Please don't limit me in how I may grow and improve! O Lord, I do want to learn and have ability to throw further, react better! Please improve my skills, coordination. O Dad, please don't let others limit me because I make mistakes and don't have a natural skill as they see it! Daddy, please teach me to play ball!   (5/9/97)]

* * * * *

My relationship with my mother is growing. It is totally different from what it has always been. Just recently, on the phone, she mentioned that she thought the reason we were getting along so well was that we weren't living together now. I'm not blaming her so much, and I'm able to just share how I'm doing, and what I'm feeling. We can just talk about things now. She admits what she did was wrong. She's even beginning to deal with her own problems.

[I had a visit from my mom. It was glorious, we prayed, cried, talked, shared, encouraged, and were open and honest unlike we had been in so long. I praise my Lord for it was a prayer answered! (5/15/95)]

Her father was a minister, and they were always concerned about what people would say or think. I heard a lot of negatives about my mother from them as I was growing up. I had my grandparents on a pedestal, but that's been shattered lately.

In 12-Steps, I began to see how my grandmother was a shopping addict. She shopped, just to shop—the way I did drugs. We both went through the same pattern of our addiction things, then we'd ask the same question, *"Why did I do that?"*

My grandparents whitewash and cover over their own stuff, but not other peoples'! They can't deal with the things I try to share with them now.

[I just watched a movie about a family fighting and squabbling over a Down syndrome child. It reminded me so much of my grandparents, mom, and my family's life—the control, evil, hatred, anger and self-righteous talk, and manipulative blame and sickness. I cried and prayed for my mom who has been so wounded by my grandparents' selfish controlling, and love based on meeting their conditions and approval, and if you don't, all you get is put downs and criticism, not support. (8/18/96)]

* * * * *

After I went to jail before coming to prison, Carol moved in with a girlfriend, then into her own apartment. She went back to her old friends who used to hang out at her mother's drinking and doing drugs.

My second son was born in November 1994. He was conceived during the period of our relapse, and was born while I was in the Salvation Army program. I had some sober time with him when he was a baby. He was about 5–6 months old when I left for prison.

[I called. It was so precious hearing my little man say, ' *I love you, Daddy!*' O Lord, it hurts so much for I am missing so much. He is talking more and more. He told me of the motorcycles and four-wheeler he rode. It touched my heart. My mom said he called the Garfield card I made him for Valentine's 'his book.' (2/19/96)]

I've only talked to Carol once since entering prison. It was in April 1995. She didn't tell me it was over between us, but she told my grandmother that. She said she wanted me to see the kids, and that it would be okay for me to write to her. I wrote a stack of them, but kept them. Now, when I read through them, I can see the stages I've gone through since then.

[I called and got my granddad. He sounded quiet. I asked how my sons were doing. He said fine, that they were in the other room. That they were not going to tell them I was calling for it seemed to upset them. I accepted that even though I believed that he was being overprotective. I was at peace and asked to talk to my grandma. The next voice I heard on the phone was Carol! I was stunned. I said, '*Hi*,' and as I began to talk, I cried. I told her I loved her. I know she cares and loves me, even though on the phone she was being kind, yet strong and self-sufficient, I gathered. I love that lady. I sensed in her more feeling and hurt that she has covered.   (12/24/95)]

Carol's with another man now, and has had another baby with him. The kids aren't being taken care of, and the house is a mess—just like it was when we were spaced out. My mother goes by. She says the house is always shut-up with the curtains pulled. There are always dishes in the sink, and cockroaches. My older son should be in school, but he can't go because he always has head lice.

[It hurts, it hurts! My heart belongs to my wife, hers mine, and she is giving herself to another! She is with another man, pregnant! It tears me up so deep inside. I so want to share my life with her, and have the privilege of her sharing hers with me. And it hurts! I'm angry because she is betraying me! Lord, why is this hurting so bad? It feels like this will kill me!   (10/26/97)]

My mother used to go erratic about the kids, when Carol and I were strung out. She would call the Child Protection Service. We learned when to anticipate the visits, and would clean everything up before they came to check us out. So, the CPS think my mother is a nut. Now, when she calls about the kids, they call Carol to tell her they're coming out. So, we can't get anything to happen for the kids. I'm thinking of writing to CPS to tell them about this. Maybe that would help.

At this point, I don't feel I can do anything for my kids. My mother and grandma keep in touch with them and Carol. I feel a lot of grief over their situation.

* * * * *

I still have hopes for Carol and my marriage. That is the deepest desire of my heart. I pray for her every day. I understand her pain and running. I've done a lot of running in my life—not wanting to face up to anything. I want her to find what I'm finding. I know I can't connect with her the way she is, and that I can't fall back into enabling.

[It's been a hard day. Right now I just finished crying so deeply with such deep pain missing Carol. At first it was hard because I can't remember many good things. There was so much sin, and in much of what we did I did not see to her needs or cares because I was so concerned for me. Yet somehow as I write I know inside I did and still do truly love her. I did care and have desires for her, but yet good intentions and feelings got nowhere in my state of no discipline, and my lack of character to live up to all I wanted to be.   (5/21/96)]

I want to have a family. I want to be a dad to my sons. Not being able to is what hurts me the most in here. I want to do for them what I didn't have—a dad to play with them, that teaches them baseball, that helps them with homework, that they can talk to. My oldest will be 9 when I get out.

If my wife doesn't change and get established, maybe I'll try to get custody. Part of me says that's impossible because of my charges, but part of me has hope. I feel God is telling me to wait and to trust. I have to hang onto him.

[O, Babe, it's hard! O God, I miss her! When my cellie was reading a letter from his girl, I hurt hearing his girl say she will love him forever no matter what. O, how I long to hear those words again from you, Carol! I remember you saying this before. I hope you still do love me, and will be able to feel and have that with me again. (7/25/95)]

* * * * *

I'm not ready yet to confront Bud with the abuse. I still love him. I'm learning that I don't have to feel "either / or" about him, or anyone, but that I can love him and be angry with him, too.

[Oh, God, I've been robbed of my dignity, self-respect and my right to be loved! Bud, why did you hurt me so much? I'm so angry at you, you told me you loved me!   (5/15/95)]

I'm talking with others, and learning to trust certain people with my shame and feelings. I feel a lot of guilt. I'm learning to face these things, and to let it all heal. I can still feel the pain—like while I'm talking right now—but it doesn't overwhelm me anymore. I'm learning that you don't handle everything all at once, but just a little at a time, as much as you can handle right now.

[As I read about acknowledging and owning the pain, I hurt. I wished I would have known and been able to get to my hurt before I hurt so many others. Reading how bad memories become more powerful the longer we keep them out of our consciousness, really gives me understanding of my life and the destruction I've brought on myself and others.   (5/28/95)]

*   *   *   *   *

I get out in 2001. While I'm here, my goals are to stay in the groups for my personal growth, to stay involved in the chapel, to finish the electronics and data processing programs, and, if I have time, to start working so I can begin saving. When I get out, I want to work in the computer industry somewhere.

I used to be afraid of the future. Drugs allowed me to just have to live in "today." Now, even though I know there are some tough things ahead, like Megan's Law (mandates notification of neighbors when a convicted sex offender moves into the neighborhood), I'm not afraid of the future. Is that hope?

* * * * * * * * * * * * *
* * * * * * * * * * * * *

I have always been afraid of drugs, and I am probably one of the few men in here who has never been drunk, or used pot or another illicit drug. I would like to present that as virtue, but, I suspect, it was the unconscious awareness of the "monster" lurking within me is—and is, perhaps, latent in all of us. What I know of drugs is what I've seen and heard around me, especially here—there are few human success stories in prison.

The dominant similarity in the stories shared in this book—as well as in those of 80% of our companions—is the disastrous role of drugs in each of them. While the steps are different which lead to the start of drug use, once that threshold has been crossed, the consequence is the same—a downhill slide into dissolution.

The lure of drugs is the seductive promise of "freedom"—from hurting, remembering, thinking, feeling—from being lost, confused, nobody, bored, ashamed. "Freedom" is exacted at a terrible cost, though, as Darcy bears witness, and extracting one's soul from its clutches is a difficult and discouraging wrestling match, even for those most sincerely committed to the battle.

It is easy to understand the addictive attraction of getting high for Darcy. There was a lot of pain to escape, and a huge void to fill at the core of his being. What is hard to believe is the "monster" which was unleashed in this quiet, meek, gentle young man, under the "freedom"

of drugs. As others have alluded, drugs create a Jekyll and Hyde personality, in which "what could have been" is almost always surrendered to
"what ought not to have been."

*   *   *   *   *

It has been two years since Darcy initially shared his story, but we are
still in daily contact. Darcy continues to hold ambivalent feelings about
the three major loves of his life: his mother, his stepbrother who
molested him, his wife. He and his mother have made great progress in
helping one another heal, and a reconciling, deepening relationship is
developing between them. While much of the residue of the past
remains, in the present, Darcy is basking in the love that eluded him
from the womb.

Bud is still the source of great confusion for Darcy. He has come to
the place where he is able to both love his stepbrother, and feel anger at
him. One day he knows he needs to confront him directly with both
feelings, but he does not have the inner-confidence and clarity yet. He
needs more time to establish his own sense of himself.

Darcy's fantasy of a "happy ever after" ending to his marriage has
gradually given way to the more realistic acceptance that what he and
Carol shared was more drug co-dependency than love. And, while
Darcy has been building a solid foundation for a new kind of future,
Carol continues lost in the hazy non-life of drugs. He knows he will
have to depend upon Carol's good will to maintain a relationship with
his children. He has not totally abandoned his Don Quixote-like holy
mission of rescuing and restoring his Desdemona.

In his ambiguous feelings regarding Carol, and in his childlike ways
of praying and speaking of his relationship with God, the boy is still in

search of the man. Darcy still lives partially in daydreams where there is magic and everything is as he wishes it were.

Yet, in very real ways, Darcy has also begun to experience in himself the "hero" of his childhood games. He has established a solid spiritual foundation, become a computer whiz, has real reason to look to his future with positive anticipation—and he has even become a credible baseball player.

* * * * *

[Not in words and not in me
but in what He has done,
a hope for a future without
fear of things to come.

A love for Him for who you
are by the mighty work he's done.
To know your part to walk
with Him and not be on the run.

To find the peace that goes
beyond the torment of the past,
to know His true and precious
love, the only love that lasts.

(Edited from a poem-prayer, 1/10/97)]

Booker—My Mentor and Guardian Angel

Booker entered the Youth Authority for the first time at age nine. He has spent at least 20 of his 39 years imprisoned, and the earliest he can hope to parole is 2032.

I first met Booker when I pounded on the wall of my cell to protest the loud music reverberating through from the neighboring cell. At the next unlock, he came to my door to apologize, and my closest prison friendship began.

Booker was raised in the Bay Area. His parents split when he was one, and his father, for whom he has mostly warm feelings, died suddenly while relatively young. He had worked as a custodian and clean-up man, and had served as a deacon in his Southern Baptist black church.

By contrast, Booker's relationship with his mother has been emotionally non-existent. There is very little contact, and he harbors a deep anger and resentment toward her, as his Mother's Day poem powerfully conveys.

At age 10, Booker went to live with an aunt, but, because she couldn't handle him, that soon led to a series of foster and group homes, and periods of incarceration. *"I don't remember ever going to school. No one made me, so I just skipped. I used to think all the problems with my family were the cause of my troubles. Now, I think it has been a lack of discipline. I guess that's probably it."*

He does tend to lead with his feelings in a compulsive way. Sometimes, by the time his head catches up, his good intentions have led to negative consequences. Among the "ghosts" that haunt him, are the memories of all the lost and never healed relationships he has sought but never grasped.

Booker entered into a hasty "need to belong to someone" marriage while in county jail a few years ago, but, after some months of passionate professions of undying love, that has moved through unanswered letters and disconnected phones to unofficial disintegration.

He has five half-siblings, only two of whom maintain any level of contact, and none of whom offer any material support. Booker has a 19-year-old son who has just begun at junior college. For years, Booker has written and handcrafted cards for him, but silence is the only response. He knows in his head that his son is angry at feeling abandoned, but his heart aches. The boy's mother sent a high school graduation announcement, and Booker managed to have a gift sent. *"I haven't heard from my son or his mother since the graduation, and I honestly don't know if he got it, or even liked it. I know I'm always saying 'No more!,' and I am honestly trying to just let go of all the struggle. It isn't easy to keep reaching out to my family and get nothing back."* In the three years I've known him, Booker has never had a visit.

I have not known Booker "the criminal." The friend I have come to know is my hurt and hurting, loyal and loving, compassionate and caring, mentor and guardian angel. He helped me learn prison ways, and protected me from its dangers. More than once, I saw him watching from the sidelines ready to jump in should I get over my head.

On his birthday in July 1998, Booker was transferred to another prison. I hosted an ice cream party for him the night before, then the two of us walked and talked until lockdown. We exchanged the words of affection and encouragement we needed to do. Since we spent time together every day, sharing our ups and downs, his absence created a real void for me. I miss him.

Usually prison-to-prison mail is not allowed, but our request was granted, so we have been able to continue sharing and supporting one another. Booker has since been "adopted" by some of my family, a widow and a nun in their 80s, and two retired men. An especially beautiful, mutually life-giving bond has grown between Mrs. Yost and Booker (he calls her Mom). She and a mutual friend helped Booker edit and bind his many poems.

Booker began writing when he was 15, but only in the past ten years has he done so seriously to release the tension. *"I write, read the Bible and make my cards so I don't go insane."* As he faces the years ahead, his goal is primarily to survive. *"I don't ever want to adjust to jail. I don't ever want to start liking it."* When we first met, I found it hard to listen to his litany of complaints. For Booker, the drinking glass of life was always half empty, but that was also his life's experience. I attempted to reflect back other ways of looking at life. Gradually, light seemed to begin permeating his usual gloom.

Booker saw his transfer as an opportunity to start over in a new place, with new people and with new ways of thinking and being. He set some new goals, and gave himself to them. A month after his move, he wrote, *"I've been putting a lot of energy into changing, and I am somewhat (humbly) impressed! Since I've been here I drink less and less coffee, use profanity almost none (and apologize when I do), and I've been praying in every prayer to help me quit smoking. I jog five laps every day. And I'm giving my efforts over to 100% faith in Jesus. It isn't easy, but neither have I been struck with any real temptations or challenges to my faith as it develops."*

Booker wears his heart on his face, which is either aglow with a toothy, squinty-eyed grin, or a don't-come-too-close frown. He wears his hair and his beard in perpetual stubble. When he laughs—which is often—he bends over and dances around. While I don't see his face in person anymore, it is vividly alive as I read his letters. He tries hard to be loving and to find love—sometimes too hard—but there is much in him which is truly lovable. Our friendship will endure.

Because of our close relationship, I did not ask Booker to be a subject for this book, but I have included some of his poems. You will come to know him through them. In November 1999, he shared how far he has come to "Filling his glass," in a beautifully expressed, wisdom-laden letter:

> *"I have learned a lot about giving and receiving from everyone I have met and learned to love through you. It has been a great testimony of forgiveness and concern for each other as human beings, encouraging each other to keep on having faith and hoping for greater things, and that the past is not always a testament of the future and what it can bring.*
>
> *"If I were to have continued, as I still sometimes do, to think in terms of how much has been lost, then there would never be any reason to think the future could ever be any different. I am still not happy with life, but spiritually, in some way I still cannot fully articulate, I somehow have hope that the things I think of (naturally and supernaturally) are very much possible.*

"I think I have learned the more the things you dream are in line with God's will, the better chance you have of those things coming true. Calling those things which be not as if they are! I don't really conceive of that fully as a reality, but more as a notion I would like to fully comprehend in God!"

* * * * * * * * * * * *

* * * * * * * * * * * *

Right Now

Right now I don't?
And what I don't know,
I am trying to find out:
Why Cool Cat's cool?
Why knowledge is king?
Why life is so defecated?
Why when you think you got something,
You find you got nothing?
Why you do it when you know better?
Why you promise when they're always unkept?
Why, when you subtract then add,
Then fractionalize and divide to find
Equation, you always come up with Zero?
Now, can someone tell me where to find
Hope? It's really all I'm looking for.
I can find all else, thank you, on my own!

Booker (8-9-96)

About Living

I got one thing to say
About living!
I wanted to,
But it lied to me.
So why the hell trust it?
It ain't kept not one promise!
Now, you dig that…

One thing to say about living—
It lies to you.
Now, can you express more truth?
I am not deceiving you—
Well, maybe I am, life's in me now.
I said more than one thing,
Or did I?

Booker (8-9-96)

An Answer to Silence—A Lesson to Love

Dear Mother!
I wrote to you recently with questions and you didn't answer? So, here
is my reply to your silence.
You brought me into the world a crying, shining, beautiful face,
A black ass smacked by protected rubber hands.
And you christened me a name I still do not know,
Partly because I do not even know you!
I have no idea what your hands feel like, the smell of your hair.
I do not recall, nor do I remember ever, your breast nipple.
I see your face and I love you, but I have never seen
My Mother in your eyes.

You never held me, you never encouraged me to
Be anything but a nobody you could use and abandon,
And allow the process to continue—and every step I have hurt,
And hurt others one after another.

Still, to this day, I have just begun to understand the
Emotional impact you have had on my life—why it is when
I try to love and be loved, I lack nurturing capability—
Because you didn't love me (but you brought me here),
And you let me down?

You brought me into this world a crying, shining, beautiful face,
And you didn't even see the Sun rising out of your womb.
Yet, you abused its light, and, now, so many have stood in
Total Darkness waiting for the precious nimble touch of your
Fingers, and the light of your teeth seeping through lips of
Optimism and tough love.

I listened so intently for your heart beat
To find rhythm—did you know, Mother, I dance very well?
Do you even care that you let me down and upset the entire
Process of my life? Or does a mother realize how many lives

She touches? how many she can love? how much "life" she
   Can produce by simply loving her own children?

I guess I should have understood I was on my own
When you said you didn't want me, but children do not
            Understand "on your own!"
        But I have found—on my own—
     I am somebody, and I am beautiful!

            I love you, and
         The Son *is* shining!

    Booker (Mother's Day, 1997)

HOPE

         I do not want to lose hope,
      But every hope I've had leaves—
       Some aloud, some very quietly,
            But leave they do.
          I do not understand this
        Empty possession of hopes!
      I'll walk a bit longer, and try to
            Not feel so empty.

          Booker (undated)

The Maker or Thing Formed?

We are all walking entities uncertain of
Tomorrows, passing yesterdays and dying in
Our nostalgias which have never been.
Receiving half filled goblets of wine,
Noticing roses as we walk by casting our
Feeble shadows upon them, for brief moments
Incapsulating all the power of the sun inside
Our bodies, it's warmth detoured around our hearts
Which are so hardened with brokenness and grief,
We fight to, but never learn to quite forget.

Human condition is that way, ever learning and
Never ever understanding the frailty of our
Strengths as invincible as they really
Don't make us...

A piece of blue paper and a dream that never came,
The heart was so willing, the mind so acquainted
With the dialogs of rhetoric,
The spirit ever calling, out beyond itself
Into the beyond and God...
DAMN IT, GOD, HEAL ME!!!

How much more of this can anyone take?
Salvation and joy, rejoicing in hymns and
Praise to the master pot Maker,
Forgive me, forgive me, please do.
Am I to feign something like joy
And happiness, dreams and accomplishment
Running when my feet have not moved one inch
Towards anything materially spiritual!

God I never want to say, "Take your time,
I'll be here when You're ready."
But am a damned fool if I don't...
Booker (5-99)

Postscript

Lewis, Armando, Curtis, Benny, Darcy and Booker are wounded men, who, in turn, have been wounders. In this, their stories are no different from yours or mine. Every human person is wounded in some way, and each of us is a wounder, as we live our everyday lives with family, friends, at work—rarely consciously or deliberately, but the wounds hurt and bleed, nonetheless.

Each of us is our history, and we act out of it, and pass it on to those our lives touch. Unless we experience a healing embrace somewhere in our story, the cycle of woundedness continues unabated. To break it requires that we turn around and squarely face our wounds and our wounders. We—not they—control the power our woundedness has over us, and—through us—over others.

The men, whose stories you've read, have choices to make, as do all of us. We cannot undo our past, but we can stop repeating it. Our history becomes our future, unless our present is redeemed. Against tremendous obstacles a few of these men have begun the long and painful process of becoming healed and healers. Most still struggle. None have given up. They inspire me.

A Meditation

Only when we place our hands into the pierced side of Jesus and touch " that wounded heart of God with these hands that hurt, punish, pull wings off flies, hammer in nails, point in scorn, and clench in hatred, can they be healed and transformed into the hands of lovers.

"...the promise God gives to *all* human hands and hearts with their frightening power to hurt and heal...is the promise that the hands of all of us wounded [wounders], held in God's heart, are forgiven, restored, transformed.

"With our hands within that heart, the wounds we carry will not become infected wounds. When we touch another in healing love and comfort, the hand and heart of Christ surrounds and empowers our hands."[30]

* * * * * * * * * * * *

The End

* * * * * * * * * * * *

---

30. Flora Slosson Wuellere, *Reach Out Your Hand, and Put It In My Side*, Weavings XIII, No. 5 (Sept./Oct. 1998):12–13.

Educational and Advocacy Resources

California

Friends Committee on Legislation of California Newsletter, 926 J St., Rm. 707, Sacramento, CA 95814-2707.

California Prison Focus. Provides educational resources and speakers on prison related issues. 2489 Mission St., Ste. 28, San Francisco, CA 94110, (415) 452-3359 and 821-6545.

Little Hoover Commission Report, Jan. 1998, *"Beyond Bars: Correction Reforms to Lower Prison Costs and Reduce Crime."* Recommendations for changes aimed at reducing prison costs and recidivism. $5.00 from the commission, 660 J St., Ste. 260, Sacramento, CA 95814.

Legislative Analyst Report, Feb. 1998, on prison and parole reforms. Contact Legislative Analyst, 925 L St., Ste. 1000, Sacramento, CA 95814, 916-322-2072.

American Friends Service Committee Criminal Justice Program, advocates and educates about jail/prison conditions, three-strikes, human rights violations, criminal justice policy. Reports and informational materials available. AFSC, 1611 Telegraph Ave., Ste. 1501, Oakland, CA 94612, 510-238-8080.

Prisoners' Rights Union. Primary goals: inform prisoners of their civil rights and to advocate on their behalf. Quarterly newspaper "The California Prisoner," $5 to prisoners/$20 others; *"California State Prisoners' Handbook,"* practical guide to sentencing, prison/parole law:

$44.60/$85; lists of services and organizations available to assist prisoners and parolees.

Prison Legal Clinic, 2020 29th St., Ste. 102, Sacramento, CA 95817, 916-737-1237. Provides summaries of legislation and laws affecting prisoners/parolees and sentencing.

Californians 2 Amend 3-Strikes (C.A.T.S.). Dedicated to amending 3-Strikes law, and advocates for prisoner and family rights. 2729 N. Bristol, Ste. B5-112, Santa Ana, CA 92706, 714-541-2073.

Families to Amend California's Three-Strikes (FACTS), 1840 So. Gaffey, #274, San Pedro, CA 90731, 213-673-7120.

Catholic Center for Restorative Justice, Office of Detention Ministry, Archdiocese of Los Angeles, 3434 Wilshire Blvd., Los Angeles, CA 90010-2241. Promotes and advocates for restorative justice and Catholic social teaching. Quarterly newsletter *"Restoring Justice."*

Pro-Family Advocates, Dedicated to preservation of family unit by protecting rights of prisoners and their families. P.O. Box 17892, Long Beach, CA 90807-7892, e-mail: profamilyadvocates@juno.com

California State Government

Office of the Governor, State Capitol, Sacramento, CA 95814, 916-445-2841, FAX 445-4633. e-mail: graydavis@governor.ca.gov.

State Senate / State Assembly, State Capitol, Sacramento CA 95814. For name or phone of specific legislator: 916-322-9900. For your local legislators, check the front of your phone book under "State." The committees which handle prison and related issues are the Senate (Assembly) Public Safety Committee.

California Department of Corrections, P.O. Box 942883, Sacramento, CA 94283-0001, (916) 445-7682.

Board of Prison Terms, 428 J Street, 6th Floor, Sacramento, CA 95814.

National

Responsibility, Rehabilitation, and Restoration: A Catholic Perspective on Crime and Criminal Justice Responsibility, a Statement of the Catholic Bishops of the United States, November 15, 2000. USCC Publications Office, 3211 Fourth St. NE, Washington, D.C., Publication No. 5-934, ISBN 1-57455-394-1.

The Other Side, 300 W. Apsley St., Philadelphia, PA 19914, (215) 849-2178. Annual subscription $29.50. Bi-monthly Christian faith-based social justice magazine.

Presbyterian Criminal Justice Program. Resources include printed and audio/visual materials on prison, death penalty and related issues. 100 Witherspoon St., Louisville, KY 40202-1396, (502) 569-5810.

Changing Lenses (1990), Howard Zehr. The basic resource and research critiquing our current retributive models of justice, from both Secular and Christian perspectives, and offering practical and philosophical restorative models for reforming our justice systems. Herald Press, Scottsdale, PA. ISBN 0-8361-3512-1.

Mennonite Central Committee, U.S. Office of Crime and Justice. Resources include printed and audio/visual materials on prison, alternatives to prison, death penalty, and related topics. P.O. Box 500, Akron, PA 17501, 717-859-3889.

The Sentencing Project. Offers technical assistance in developing alternative sentencing programs; conducts research on criminal justice issues; advocates for change in the way Americans think about crime and punishment; resources for defense attorneys. Write for list of reports and publications. TSP, 918 F St., NW, Ste. 501, Washington, D.C. 20004, 202-628-0871.

The National Prison Project Journal. Quarterly journal of reports, articles, legal analysis, legislative news, developments in corrections and criminal justice fields. Annual subscription $3 prisoners/$30 others. NPPJ, 1875 Connecticut Ave., NW, Ste. 410, Washington, D.C., 20009.

Sojourners, 2401 15th St., NW, Washington, D.C. 20009. Annual subscription $30. Christian grassroots network for personal, community and political transformation, applying faith to social justice awareness and action.

9 780595 176748